Redemption in Brooklyn

Redemption in Brooklyn

The Extraordinary Lengths God Will
Go to Draw You Near to Him

Eddy Mastellone

RESOURCE *Publications* • Eugene, Oregon

This book is dedicated to all families
who have lost loved ones due to drug addiction.

Contents

Acknowledgments

Special thanks to:

Paula Moss—I thank God for gifted teachers.

Don Moss, for encouragement and friendship.

Elliot Goldenberg, for invaluable help and direction.

Diana Autin, for believing in me.

Keith Heffner, for putting the idea into my head that I should write a memoir.

Wendi and my three sons, Phillip, George, and Michael, for loving me the way you do.

An incredibly special thanks to my friend Dion. I am honored by your trust over the years and the immeasurable guidance you have shown me.

My Lord Jesus, for grace in my life, God's redemption at Christ expense.

I want to thank everyone at Wipf and Stock Publishers, from Matt Wimer to gifted editor Kara Barlow, and all those that added their special expertise to this book. What I envisioned in my heart is what you all made a reality in this book; God bless you all.

Introduction

THE NUMBER OF FAMILIES that have been tragically torn apart because of alcohol and drugs is staggering. When disappointed because of unanswered prayers, people in general tend to think that God has let them down; the church has let them down. This way of thinking is especially true of those that have issues with addictions.

When you have been sad for so long that when something bad happens, you don't cry, you just sit there and feel numb, baffled by the silence of God. We all have seasons of doubt and frustration. The good news is that God loves you; he is not mad at you, and he is not out to get you. If that were his desire, you would have been done a long time ago. As Bishop Robert Barron notes, "When it comes to the offenses that we have received from others, we are, all of us, great avatars of justice. We will remember every insult, every snub, and every shortcoming when it comes to our being hurt by others."[1] God is *not* like that!

Redemption in Brooklyn is my journey of how God helped me resolve the many issues I had in my life: drug addiction, unforgiveness, distrust of friends that really cared about me, thoughts of suicide, compulsion to do the wrong and not the right. There were

1. Barron, "Tuesday, March 22," para. 1.

times that I thought, "Why isn't God making this all go away?" Finally, I realized I was enslaved to powers I couldn't compete against. I needed to be rescued from this despair. God did rescue me from being held in captive by darkness and despair.

I hope this memoir will inspire you to develop the ability to see God in your life by the time you finish reading this book. Be assured that God has never left you to figure it all out on your own. He has always been with you; in fact, he is with you right now.

CHAPTER 1

On My Way Home

So, THERE I WAS in a 1977 leisure suit that had been fashionable for the last two years, standing in twenty-degree weather in front of a bus station on Route 86, near Clinton Correctional Facility (known as Dannemora). I had a winter coat to wear, but I wanted to breath in the fresh air. Having been released from state prison with a life sentence, I wanted to experience every bit of fresh air and freedom I could.[1] No longer confined or restricted, I could go anywhere I wanted to go, to any place—I just had to let my parole officer know. I was free again; I had already given thought to the things I wanted to stay away from. There were things that would be very toxic to me, such as hanging out with old friends who were still into doing dangerous, immoral things, including taking and selling drugs. I was noticeably confident that I was about to do life on my own terms instead of being led around by someone's hand like I was blind.

---

1. Because of a change in the law, my life sentence for having had cocaine in my possession changed to a sentence of one to three years, so I was able to go on with my life without parole hanging over me. See Wilson, "Rockefeller Drug Laws."

Redemption in Brooklyn

I stood there, waiting for the big Greyhound bus to take me back to New York City, back to the old neighborhood. I came back to live with my father on Onderdonk Avenue in Ridgewood, Queens, the neighborhood I grew up in. My mother had passed away some five years earlier, so it was good to spend time with him, and he with me. It was also good for me to be accountable to someone, even if it was my father. I was working in a supermarket at the time, and after a while, I decided it was time to move out and get my own place closer to where I worked. Park Slope, Brooklyn, seemed to be the best place. It was affordable then, with streets lined with brownstone buildings, one right after another. Prospect Park was a couple of blocks away and the place to be on Sunday to feel like you were somewhere else other than the heart of a major city.

I made some new friends who were musicians and who loved the same kind of music that I did. They taught me how to write songs and helped me to enjoy my own style of playing. Robbie helped me to gain confidence and be comfortable with singing a song in front of people. One of my first exciting events was performing for vacationers on the island of Martinique. I was so motivated by the beauty of the island that I wrote and recorded the song called "The Sands of Martinique"—I thought it was a hit and sent it off to a few record companies. I continued to write and play music; with a lot of enthusiasm and self-assurance, I was flying high. I had played at a couple of local clubs, and my social life had become remarkably busy, with parties, get-togethers, and special events. I loved the attention so much that as a result, I found my sobriety starting to suffer. It happened so slowly that I did not even realize it until it was gone! I still had my apartment, and I still had my job, but I knew addiction was beginning to take hold of me—the same old heroin.

I was seeing my parole officer once every month, and if he suspected I was doing drugs again, I would be back to finishing out my life sentence. I immediately went to a methadone therapy clinic for counseling. I decided to isolate myself from my musician friends and anyone that smoked or did drugs. I started to reach out to a close trusted friend.

Jack was a successful businessman and seemed to have his life in order. While giving me a ride home from work one night, we sat there in his car in front of my apartment on Eighth Avenue and President Street in Park Slope, Brooklyn, discussing where our lives were at. We both talked about nearing thirty years old and whether we wanted to continue breaking up with girlfriends over stupid reasons. So, we both purposed to generally start caring for someone new that would enter our lives.

Now, I would like to believe that at seven years old, when I witnessed my grandmother Matilda praying in Italian for God to send spouses to her grandchildren that would lead them to heaven, I didn't have faith to believe that or understand what that prayer meant. But now nearing thirty years old, I was not sure if it was possible until Wendi walked into my life that day in the supermarket. There were six men behind the counter as Wendi walked in with her sister Suzanne. Suzanne was extremely attractive and flamboyant. She attracted all the attention in the place except mine. My eyes were on Wendi; I was watching her every move. She was pleasant but not flirtatious, attractive in a very strikingly natural way, with self-assurance. The contrast between Wendi and her sister was as wide as the Grand Canyon. As she responded to my question of "Can I help you?" she was the picture of confidence, as I stood there wonder struck. Her youngest son, George, was with her, and I observed that for a five-year-old, he was friendly and respectful, which attracted me even more to Wendi.

The next few weeks, we kept running into each other in the neighborhood. There was one evening that changed it all for me. I was on the subway platform and was spotted by Wendi and her sister Suzanne, who were on the opposite side of the train station. Suzanne yelled out loud, "She likes you." Wendi stood there mortified.

After hearing that Wendi liked me, the next time I saw her I used the opportunity to invite her to accompany me to a barbecue on the Fourth of July, which was the following week. When the day came, it was raining and the event was cancelled, so instead we went to dinner and a movie. We had a lot of fun and enjoyed each other's company very much. Cautiously optimistic was what we both secretly felt—I was sure of it. Romance is always exciting and scary in the beginning. Over a few weeks' time, I got to spend time with her and her two young sons. George was a natural charmer and a very likable child, whereas Phillip was more reserved but friendly and respectful. To watch the interaction between them was to conclude that they obviously liked each other. I have learned that you can love someone but not really like them. That was not the case here—they not only liked each other but had a deep, protective love for each other. As I continued to spend time with them, I made sure that I remained on my best behavior. I had a tendency to sound like Rocky Balboa and it was a fight not to, but I won out. I was so impressed with their little family that I was slowly yearning to play a bigger part in it. Wendi was so genuine in her approach to life around her, never giving me a reason to doubt her sincerity—there was no pretense at all. I knew right where she stood with her children, with me, and with her faith.

One time, she asked me if I believed in Jesus; I said yes. Then she asked me if I believed in reincarnation, and I said yes. You would have thought I would have a handle on spiritual matters, but what I had was a lot of different ideas of philosophy mixed up in a blender. Her response was very caring. She asked why, if you believe in one, you need the other. Such a simple question to most people, but I had an epiphany over it. I am embarrassed now about how little depth of understanding I had on the subject. I started wondering how I knew so little about a religion I had participated in as a young boy. I started to think about what I remembered I had read or heard during Mass. I remembered what the priest had said during my marriage ceremony ten years earlier—that a man leaves his father and mother and is united to his wife, and they become one. I had already experienced two people who had agreed to be of one mind and soul but who remained halves, and it wound up being a living hell. Just because you are married doesn't mean you're ready and that you have arrived at maturity. Happiness is not finding the right person; happiness is being the right person.

So, I started putting all my energy and thought into being focused on bringing happiness and stability to Wendi, Phillip, and

George. My life up till then had been the world revolving around me. I was ready for someone else to be the center of my universe. I think I found the boys so delightful because they were raised to respect adults. Wendi was in her early teens when her family uprooted from New Jersey and moved to an island in the Caribbean Sea. She married there and had two sons, Phillip and George.

Are you a victim or are you a survivor of your experiences? What am I willing to leave behind from the place I called home, and what am I willing to enthusiastically embrace of a foreign influence? My grandparents faced the same questions when leaving Naples, Italy, on a ship with their children to Ellis Island, now a former immigration station.

CHAPTER 2

Early Roots

GENNARO MASTELLONE CAME TO the United States with his wife, Matilda, in the year 1910. They brought their seven sons and four daughters with them from Naples, Italy. They arrived on Ellis Island in New York City and began their life journey in New York City as American citizens. Shortly after they arrived, Matilda gave birth to another son, Ralph—my father.

My grandfather was a hard worker, doing whatever he had to do to put food on the table. So, my father and his brothers learned at an early age what a strong work ethic meant; it meant that you lived and did not die. Their hopes and dreams for a better life gave them the endurance and persistence to persevere. The determination to be somebody was something that most immigrants wanted. My grandfather was no different, no matter how much blood, sweat, and tears it took to achieve that goal he had of being somebody.

In the present day, being Italian can be extremely attractive to people. Speaking with a sexy accent, dressing in chic clothing, maybe driving a Maserati looks very cool, never mind the Italian cuisine. However, it was not always like that. Newly arriving Italians were treated worse than stray dogs. Often-degrading labor conditions were just a stepping-stone to acceptance and legitimacy within American society. Basically, my grandparents suffered and endured the hardship so that their children and grandchildren would have a better life.

Racial prejudice was the norm. Italians were mostly arriving from southern Italy; they were physically darker than other immigrants coming from Europe. It was not uncommon for them to be hanged by mobs in Southern states, especially around New Orleans. Their Catholic faith also put them at odds with Protestant Americans. It was easy for local law enforcement to blame crimes on men who did not know English or their legal rights as American citizens.

The Italian anarchists Ferdinando Sacco and Bartolomeo Vanzetti were tried and executed in 1927 in what was a prime example of anti-Italianism. Due to the radical political views of these two Italian immigrants, they were put to death for crimes neither committed. Despite their alibis, the evidence, and public support, they were still executed in the electric chair. The trial is still studied today as a case study in civil liberties, as it is obvious that anti-Italian feelings were rampant among both the jury and the judge.[1] Folk singer Joan Baez told the story passionately in one of her songs, called "The Ballad of Sacco and Vanzetti." Seeing the world as it is and knowing where you come from puts everything else into perspective.

My mother and father married in October of 1944. Dorothy was nineteen years old and Ralph was thirty-two years old. During the next ten years, they and their four children were a typical, average-income family. My father worked two jobs while my mother stayed at home to take care of the household chores, the children, and the finances. Because there were no credit cards then, life was a lot simpler. Aside from the mortgage on the family home, most families then were debt free. During that time, it was a family affair, with two-parent households of a mom and a dad. Divorce was not a common thing because of social pressure. You were supposed to get married and stay married, no matter how

---

1. See "Sacco & Vanzetti"; Wikipedia, s.v. "Sacco and Vanzetti," https://en.wikipedia.org/wiki/Sacco_and_Vanzetti.

miserable you both were. Divorce carried a stigma back then that most people wanted to avoid.

After dinner, the family would watch TV, if they had one. The whole family watched the same show; only having one television in the home, you had no choice. One TV, one telephone, one radio, one record player.

When I became old enough to go to school, my mother changed my name from Espedito to Edward. She told me it was because she did not want me to be bullied by other kids. Perhaps it was because she had heard from my grandparents about their experience when they had first arrived from Italy, or because she had read in the newspaper about the experiment they did in the 1940s called the "doll test." It was a psychological experiment designed to test the degree of marginalization caused by prejudice and the perception we have of others and ourselves. Children can be cruel to one another when someone is odd, or when someone does not look the same or act the same as they do.[2]

We moved around a lot due to rising rents or because my dad wanted us to live in a better neighborhood. Living in the Bushwick neighborhood of Brooklyn was a bit of a culture shock. South of where we lived was the Black side of town, and West of us was the Hispanic area of town. The northeast section of Bushwick was where we lived, the White side of town. After moving there, I learned about racism, bigotry, and judging people by their color and economic status. I wanted to fit in and be accepted, and I did what was expected of me to fit in. Thankfully, drugs were not in the equation—that came later. What was expected of me was to degrade someone because of their ethnic background by assaulting them physically and verbally, the very thing my mother did not want me to face with a name like Espedito.

But I wanted to be known, to be noticed as one of the guys. Acceptance was what I was driven to acquire. The neighborhood norm was to be respected at all cost. At thirteen years old, it was overly exciting to take chances and live dangerously by knowingly breaking the law. A lot of times, I would see the same guys that I

2. For more information about the "doll test," see "Brown v. Board."

was trying to degrade in the gang fights the next day in school, as if nothing had ever happened. Well, that all changed the day I was surrounded by every Black kid in the school at lunchtime. I realized that my time in the confessional might pay off if they murdered me, but suddenly, "Big Red" parted the sea of kids that had the kill look written on their faces. He was a light-skinned Black man about six foot five with red hair. He put his arm around me and told them to leave me alone and walked me back from the schoolyard into the school building. My dad was not a bigot, and I guess "Big Red" noticed that about my father every time he bummed a cigarette from him on the corner of Schaefer and Central Avenue. He knew that I was his son, and I believe that is why he rescued me.

~

A couple of weeks later, we moved to Ridgewood, Queens. Unlike the Brownsville and Bushwick sections of Brooklyn, Ridgewood was like a small town outside of the city. Cobblestone streets, buildings that were built in the design of those in Europe, so much character and tasteful design. Overlooking the area was the Highland Park Reservoir, a great place to view the New York City skyline. I spent several Halloween nights up there and in the surrounding cemeteries. We had to make our own fright night among the gravestones. Experiencing the intense feeling of fear as someone jumped out of the shadows with a loud scream was great fun.

There were no empty lots or burnt-out buildings in this neighborhood. Everyone took pride in where they lived, whether they owned or rented. Seeing someone in the morning out scrubbing the stairs to the entrance of their home with soap and water was not an uncommon experience. Wyckoff Avenue between Myrtle and Fresh Pond Road was my Times Square. We had the RKO Madison Theatre, which had 2700 seats. The grand foyer was two stories high and had a vaulted ceiling with a crystal chandelier, and its walls were of colored marble with bronze borders. Leading to the mezzanine promenade was a super-wide marble staircase that brought patrons to a lounge area with restrooms and other facilities. The large auditorium included a huge balcony with private box seating overlooking the stage. In front of the large stage was an orchestra pit with three separate elevators—one for the orchestra, one for the lights, and one for the piano and Wurlitzer organ, which was an unusual extravaganza for a neighborhood theater. The theater opened in November of 1927 and closed sometime in early 1978.[3] I like to think of it as our neighborhood's very own Radio City Music Hall, which was built five years after the RKO Madison Theatre. I saw a lot of celebrities there while they were promoting their latest movie; it was like a Hollywood premiere. There was no doubt that these movie stars were special, and we all wanted to be one of them. A kid like me dreamed of having adoration like they got.

Junior high school was, for me, everything not having to do with education. It was about friends and feeling like I meant something to the world around me. I knew my parents loved and cared for me, but that was all unconditional. I soon realized that it was not that way when I stepped out into the neighborhood, because there, everything was conditional. If you wanted respect, you had to act tough; you had to earn it. If you wanted to be popular with the girls, you had to be cool, to appear confident and self-assured and to look the part. I would jump into the skin of James Bond when I had to. Even on Wednesday afternoons at 1:00 p.m., when I would go to Saint Mathias Catholic Church for religious instructions, I was playing a part.

I learned about all the saints that were in heaven, and they were all up there, but we had a patron saint here on earth who was the earthly protector of all of us who were feeling like we were alone, and that was Dion DiMucci. He sang about disappointments, loneliness, and insecurities in songs like "Lonely Teenager," "Somebody Nobody Wants," "Runaround Sue," and "The Wanderer" who was as happy as a clown knowing that the clown mask hides how sad he really is. I was wearing the James Bond mask and could identify with the clown. Dion was my silent friend keeping my secret. It was quite easy to stand in front of the mirror and sing those songs and feel like $1,000,000. I do not think that a therapist

3. See "RKO Madison Theatre," para. 1.

could have done any more to help a young male kid. Music started to take hold of me and steer me into how I saw the world around me, my family, my church, my school, my friends, and my life. When the Beatles came along, the girls loved them but the macho guys like me resisted. But I think most of us came around to being big fans.

CHAPTER 3

Coming of Age

THE LATE '60S WERE great for me. Long hair, beautiful hair—there are no words for the beauty, the splendor, the wonder of any hair! I was able to grow my hair long and hide my big elephant ears that I was so self-conscious about. The macho men who were close friends were not having any part of the changing trends. Just a couple of months earlier, I had been just like them, and now, I was being referred to as anything but a macho male. The excitement for a seventeen-year-old like myself was in the city, Manhattan—Greenwich Village with its popular cafés, jazz clubs, restaurants (like Shakespeare's), and the Fillmore East; Midtown Manhattan, where there were a lot of dance clubs, like the Cheetah on Fifty-Third Street and Broadway. My favorite was the Electric Circus at Saint Marks Place in the East Village.

A weekend night would start off by meeting all my friends at Groveland Billiards on St. Nicholas Avenue in Ridgewood. People dancing and a jukebox rocked the pool hall. You could hear songs about making a world full of love, about social justice, about finding peace, or about protesting the Vietnam War. Those songs helped to deal with life's frustration at the age we were all at, and marijuana mellowed that aggressive tendency to respond violently when reasoning was nowhere to be found. I know marijuana is deemed the gateway drug; for me, it was a gateway into alternative ways of thinking with my mind. I was not alone in this. There were some looking to Eastern religions—some following Swami Satchidananda, a Hindu religious teacher; some following ancient oracles of Chinese philosophers which taught how to be one with nature and the universe.

There came along Dr. Timothy Leary, who I met in a brownstone building on the Lower East Side of Manhattan one night. While sitting on the floor, a number of us gathered to hear him talk about how to turn on, turn in, and drop out. "Turn on" meant to experiment with hallucinogens such as LSD. It made him the bogeyman of the establishment. I wanted so desperately to understand who I was and where I needed to go to get answers. It was all very new to me; I was not an intellectual. My way of communicating was through three expressions: "What's up?" "Yo, hey," and "What's happening?" So, I began to become intrigued; my curiosity was becoming aroused about things I had not heard about before. Discovering these secrets to life that I had thought no one knew, because no one talked about them, was extremely exciting to me.

My confidence level began to reach new heights. I began to like the East and West Villages more and more, spending all my free time there. So, at the end of 1966, I left Ridgewood, Queens, and moved to Lexington Avenue and Thirty-Sixth Street in Manhattan. The music scene was exploding; there were so many venues for singer-songwriters to play their music, like The Bottom Line, The Bitter End, and Cafe Wha? What you experienced at those places were musicians who had not yet become experienced enough to be polished performers, but you enjoyed them because of that and because of their innocence. The Electric Circus was another place; it became the ultimate mixed-media pleasure dome, with dancing and live bands. When I met Sly and the Family Stone and The Chambers Brothers, they were giants compared to The Chambers Brothers' drummer, Brian Keenan, who was my height. The Chambers Brothers, all being six foot four and me being five foot eight, seemed like they could touch the sky with their music, and they did.

Besides featuring these awesome musicians, the place amplified the excess of drugs that characterized the '60s. Security was a biker's club called The Aliens which worked every night. It was happening at 1925 Saint Marks Place, and people filled the streets, making it feel like it was Mardi Gras every night. This place was strange inside; the walls were not at a right angle to the floor, which—combined with strobe lights and swirling crowds—made for delightfully disorienting experiences.

The Fillmore East was a great place to see bands live—some known and some not so known. The Allman Brothers Band played so many shows that they were called the house band. I saw them so many times there, along with the Grateful Dead, Jimi Hendrix, and Janis Joplin. Janis was not even on the marquee when I saw her; it was just Big Brother and the Holding Company. I sat in the middle of the second row; Janis was directly in front of me with a pint of Southern Comfort next to the microphone stand. Her voice overshadowed her appearance. That was the first time I had ever heard a woman sing with such soul and depth in my life, something I will never forget. You could talk to the performers back then. But after Woodstock happened, at a music event you could not get within ten feet of them. Like Timothy Leary—I sat next to him on the floor and listened to him talk, and a couple of months later, he—like Bob Dylan and the rest—became like gods. We hung on every word they said; they knew the secrets of life. It is almost embarrassing when I think about how naive we were. It is said that "ignorance is bliss"—I was very blissful. I could spend every waking hour walking around the West Village and going into the small clothing boutiques with the latest mod fashion, music shops, etc.

There was, on the surface, a sense of innocence in the air, but I am sure there was something or somebody working in the darkness to take advantage of the trusting nature of the young minds of my generation. As things got weirder, I began to expect the unusual and found myself willing to tolerate the existence of opinions or behaviors that I did not necessarily agree with. That went on for a while, until I felt I needed to get back to some normality in my life.

I began dating a girl from the old neighborhood of Ridgewood, where I had spent some of my early teenage years. Susan was the same age as me—eighteen years old by then. After a few months had gone by, Susan moved in with me, more for a reason of convenience. Yes, we were attracted to each other, and the conditions were very favorable for her to live in Manhattan. She had previously lived in the borough of Queens but worked in Manhattan, so she could basically walk to work now, and I was tired of the dating scene—someone different every night became challenging. After moving in together, our relationship began to become more traditional for a time. We were living paycheck to paycheck. One day, we bought a ticket from a church raffle at St. Brigid's church bazaar and won $5,000. In our childlike mindset, we thought we were set for life. I suggested that we should move back to Ridgewood and get married.

Chapter 4

The Perfect Storm

WE FOUND A ONE-BEDROOM apartment off Fresh Pond Road and began to become acclimated to living in the old neighborhood where we both grew up. We were married now but kept the same unmarried friends. It was cool to do that, because we were cool. We were married and were now seen as mature—our relationship had proceeded to the heights of being perfect, because we had made a commitment of marriage. I accepted the modern ultratraditional lifestyle as I began to become more domesticated, while she became less. I could not see it then, but her commitment to our marriage was wavering.

At that time—the late '60s—the popular culture worked against anything that was traditional. The counterculture was in full bloom, with songs like "Love the One You're With." For my age group, the word "love" in the song was a substitute for the word "sex." As time went on, we became more and more estranged from each other, until she wanted a divorce. I felt so distant from my core values as a member of an Italian family, where no one ever got a divorce. I felt I had not only disgraced my family but also myself.

Ashamed and feeling betrayed, I started medicating myself with whatever I could get—alcohol or any kind of drugs—eventually becoming addicted to heroin. My parents did not know any of this, and because of their culture, I was viewed as a failure, so I saw no need to add to that by revealing that I was a heroin addict and homeless. The YMCA became my new home at eight dollars a night. Since it was seventy degrees inside and twenty-eight degrees outside, I was glad I was not homeless. I remember I was always feeling cold—more like freezing. On the radio, you heard Sinatra's song "That's Life"—it was on the top-ten list, so you could hear it four to five times an hour.

You would think by now that I would be experiencing shame or even concern for what my parents would feel if I overdosed and died, but I did not. I could not afford those kinds of feelings; I was desperate to get my next shot of heroin, my next high. I knew that I was out of control, so I made a call to a drug hotline. The lady who was answering the hotline worked for Dr. Marie Nyswander and made me an appointment to come in and talk with her.

Back in 1964, Dr. Vincent Dole and Dr. Marie Nyswander started research on a maintenance program for heroin addicts using dolophine/methadone. I met with her, and I remember her being so kind and compassionate to me; she immediately took me as a patient. I felt truly fortunate, and I thought maybe this could be the way out. I was still thinking that despite all my faults, I was young and had plenty of time to get it right—yet, resolving my addiction to heroin and never using it again was not even considered. Under Dr. Marie Nyswander's care, my focus began to change from a desperate need for a fix to wanting a more stable way of living and wanting to not deteriorate into a drug-induced coma. I guess you could say I was disconnected from my family but not from the bad influence of my friends.

I got a job driving a taxicab on the night shift. Seeing New York at night was exciting, because I was getting paid to go all over the five boroughs. I had quite a few celebrities in the yellow cab, and they were all genuinely nice to me. The negative side was the stress of knowing that anyone I picked up could rob me at gunpoint. Most of my fares were good, and my street smarts made me able to predict what would be dangerous. Cab drivers try to beat out the other cab drivers before they can get to the person on the curb. The consequence of being selective is that you lose money but not your life.

As I started to get more in control of my life, I met a young lady named Allison who was more like a little girl, very impressionable and very needy. She always felt like there was something wrong in her life and that she needed someone or something to fix it. I found out later that she was seeing a therapist and needed someone to talk to, and that was okay, because there were times that I was very needy. I hid behind a facade of strength and confidence when I felt like a failure for real.

Allison had grown up in an upscale neighborhood near Little Neck Bay, a very safe place to live with a little-village feel which only celebrities could afford, one of the best places to live in New York City, ranked as one of the most expensive housing markets. I was out of my social class, and her parents reminded her of that every day. Years later, I would write a letter to her parents telling them how sorry I was for the grief and emotional pain I caused them.

After dating a while, Allison and I moved in together. Her parents, naturally, were disturbed and were against it to the point of disowning her. We were okay for a couple of months until being disconnected from her parents took its toll on her. The tragic shame of it caused her to try to take her own life. It was afterward that I found out that she suffered from extreme bouts of depression and that she'd had a close relationship with her parents until I came along and disrupted their lives.

For several years, I felt tremendous guilt for being the catalyst of someone almost taking their own life. I started medicating myself again to the point of becoming a walking zombie. I could no longer function at a basic-living level—I couldn't get up to go to work or make something to eat, etc. Having no desire or foresight about the future, I was living in the present drug haze that I had made for myself.

At that time, I was living on 69th Street and Madison Avenue, and I found myself visiting those old historic churches that was sandwiched between huge skyscraper buildings. The doors of the churches were never locked back then, and I would walk up to the front pew and sit down. While sitting there for hours, I would remember as a young boy feeling the sanctity and reverence in the chapel and being close to the God of my boyhood. Sitting there, I realized how much I missed that and did not know how to get back; I had lost my way.

CHAPTER 5

I Have Lost My Way

I STILL HAD A number of unsavory people I knew that were living dangerously. I had never been arrested, and I was not worried about being associated with drug dealers, because for a first offence I would get a slap on the wrist, so I didn't care about consequences until I got stopped by the police with one ounce of cocaine. Governor Nelson Rockefeller had launched his campaign to toughen New York drug laws. He called for something unheard of: a mandatory prison sentence of fifteen years to life for drug dealers and addicts, even for those with small amounts of marijuana, cocaine, or heroin. The results were that I was on my way to serving a life sentence. First, I was sent to Sing Sing Correctional Facility, and then, a couple of months later, I was sent to Dannemora.

As I started out in my new frontier, this gated community of Sing Sing, I was being forced to coexist with all kinds of ethnic groups, and I realized how much I detested them—and now I had to live with them. At first, I thought it beneath me to talk with anyone—after all, I was not evil; I just wanted to feed my addiction. I did not kill anyone. I came close a couple of times to killing myself from an overdose. In the cell next to me was someone named Eric, who I found to be a reliable and nice guy. He was no different from me. He had the same type of friends; he liked the same kinds of things that I did—except the big difference was that I was in prison because of drugs, and he was there for murdering a city councilman's brother. I got to know him first, before I found that out. We were at a part of Sing Sing that they called the flats. They were not the big airplane-hangar-type cellblocks. Each floor had thirty cells that faced each other, and during the day, the prison guards would let us out of the cell to stretch and walk around, while they watched us.

Eric and I would sit on the concrete floor in front of our cells and talk about what had led us to being there. One time when we were sitting there, I saw in the distance something that disturbed me. It was a prison guard allowing an inmate to go in and out of everyone's cells. As they came close to me, I could see that the inmate was about six foot five and had a tattoo of a dotted line that was red, and it said "Cut Along Dotted Line." It looked every bit menacing. I remember asking the prison guard what was going on. He said this inmate with the tattoo had had items stolen from his cell. Several cartons of cigarettes and other items. Cigarettes were like having cash that you could gamble with or use to trade for illegal items that were smuggled into the prison. Your cell was the only place that was off limits to everyone but you and the prison guard. So, while this inmate was allowed by other inmates to go into the cells to look for his stuff, I was not going to allow this to happen with my cell. I said to the inmate that he had to move on to the next cell, because I did not have his stuff, and he would have to believe me. If you defy an inmate that has just been ripped off and is looking for his stuff back, you can expect that something bad is going to happen to you. But nothing did happen. There must have been a guardian angel watching over me. If I were to sum up what I learned from my experience, it was that I better make sure I did not jeopardize my ability to continue to keep breathing. I still had family that was hoping to see me again. I knew that my family still cared for and loved me by the letters I received from them. While writing to them one day in the cafeteria where inmates ate their meals, I watched with my back up against the wall as several Black and Hispanic men walked in. Being the only one in the room, I was overly concerned. I had grown up thinking that these people were different from me because of my race and because I had feelings and cared about people, and these people (I had thought) did not—they didn't care about anybody. They could not shed a tear over anything. Talk about being delusional and paranoid—I was about to face some serious reality.

They could not write letters, but I could. They had watched me for weeks going into the cafeteria and writing letters. It was a couple of weeks before Christmas, and they needed to write home. They asked me if I would write for them, and I agreed, reluctantly.

As I put down their words, I could clearly see and feel their hurts, embarrassments, and pain as their tears dripped down their faces. It was like a mirror image of myself. I started to soften up inside, because I realized that these men had the same feelings toward their families as I had. They could not go home for the holidays either, and they were bawling their eyes out over it. Sitting there listening and writing their feelings down on paper for them started to chip away in a major way at the brick wall of hate I had built.

Now, I do not want to deceive anyone or imply that this place basically was just a reform school of sorts, because it was not—far from it. It was a state penitentiary with hardened criminals that were murderers, rapists, career gangsters, and plain tortured souls. Somehow, it was like there was an invisible wall that kept me separate from those extremes.

I spent the rest of my time locked up learning about music. I taught myself how to play the guitar. I had a left-handed Yamaha FG-160 that I had specially ordered from Manny's Music on West 48th Street in Manhattan just before I had to go to prison. I'd heard so many kinds of music growing up. My father would play and sing to Mario Lanza records, while at other times, my mother played and sang to Jimmy Rogers and Bobby Darin records. We did not have iTunes then, just transistor radios, and we would sing along to the songs as we moved through the neighborhood. All these songs were in my DNA and so much a part of me. So, it was much easier to learn how to play a guitar with these old memories of songs still in my head.

CHAPTER 6

New Life from a Dead Place

As my love for Wendi and the boys grew, we both realized we wanted to be a family forever. We both left our apartments and moved to a new one at 96 Prospect Place in Park Slope, Brooklyn. Just off the corner of Flatbush Avenue and four flights up was our new apartment. It was a newly renovated brownstone building. Everything in our apartment was new. For us, it was a new beginning—a new neighborhood, new friends, and a whole new life. Work can bring fulfillment, but it pales in comparison to the enduring happiness you can find in the intimate relationships that you cultivate with your family and close friends. There are some people who would say it is not necessary, but it mattered to me, and the more something matters, the harder it is to measure.

Our first Christmas together was so memorable. We went to Christmas Mass at St. Augustine's Roman Catholic Church. Phillip and George made their Holy Communion there, and Michael was baptized there. I always found the big cathedral churches and the reverence that everyone felt because this was God's house to be so inspiring. We celebrated the day with family and our new neighbors who had arrived from Ann Arbor, Michigan, a couple of months before. Because they lived right below us, it made it easy to become good friends. Diana and Keith had an innocence about them that I was not used to. They did not talk with the street lingo, they did not appear to be high on drugs, and they were not involved in organized crime. Eventually, I found out that having come from a college town, there were only three seasons for them: football, basketball, and the art fair. The town had a music festival from May to mid-August that I would have been at every day. Diana and I had the love of music as our common ground. Anything but disco was fair ground for us to spontaneously break into a song in unison. We enjoyed our singing together so much that we went as far as recording a couple of songs in the recording studio, which was great fun. Wendi and I found both Diana and Keith very endearing, and we liked them a lot from the very beginning. Now I don't know what they were thinking when they first met me. To them, I could have been another hoodlum trying to straighten out his life, like the ones they had read about in a college-town newspaper. Judging by their actions, it wasn't like that. Their acceptance of me and the love they showed me and my new family helped me to be bold in how I loved and gave me the courage to do that. We are all afraid to say too much, to feel too deeply, to let people know what they mean to us. We ruin what could be the beauty of our lives by desensitizing ourselves to everyday interactions with family and friends. As I look back now, I know that it was not by accident that they moved to an apartment one floor beneath us—that it was by design, predetermined and ordained to enrich our journey through life.

~

It was a surprise for us during a visit to the doctor's to find out that Wendi was going to have a child. My anxiety was kept to a minimum thanks to Wendi—this was not her first rodeo, but it was mine! Most couples feel like the waiting period of a pregnancy is never going to end. I remember Wendi writing different numbers on a pad and me thinking she must have been so bored waiting for the pregnancy to be over. Suddenly, it occurred to me that she was about to go into labor and that she was counting the intensity of the contractions. I called the taxi service, and we were on our way to Caledonian Hospital in Flatbush, Brooklyn.

It was not long before Wendi was in labor and the nursing staff brought her into the delivery room. Wendi was not supposed to be in labor for over eight hours. So, when the moment came and I saw the pain that she was going through, it was overwhelming for me to watch. Dr. Lee Lim threatened to sedate me. Having never witnessed something like that, I was visibly shaken. After a long, hard labor, Michael was born. What an amazing time—if that does not unite you together; if you don't have an enormous amount of gratitude toward your baby's mother, then I feel sorry for you, because you have missed not only the wonder but the beauty of it all.

Michael was only a month old when we all got on a plane to visit Wendi's mom so she could meet her new grandson. We stayed a week, and I loved it. Growing up in New York City, we all had a sense of what it meant to succeed in life. To me, it was to retire to Florida. Well, I did not want to wait to retire there, so I started planning my escape immediately after we got back to Brooklyn. The reality was that it would not happen for another six years. Diana and Keith took Phillip and George on trips to Martha's Vineyard, museums, and cultural events that they still remember to this day as like being on field trips from school. Having new experiences exposed them to new ideas and new cultures that affected their way of seeing the world for years to come. Wendi and I will be eternally grateful.

I was learning how impressionable children are. You start thinking to yourself about life, faith, morality, and mortality—the bedrock of virtues you were brought up with and how right or wrong they are. The next couple years were exciting as a family and with our extended family, Diane and Keith. Together, we enjoyed the Macy's Thanksgiving Day Parade, Central Park, and the Bronx Zoo firework shows. The city that I had struggled to find my place in was starting to reward me with all these great experiences.

From early on, Michael experienced severe allergies. He would cry all night long and have vomiting and diarrhea, and eventually, he had to be repeatedly hospitalized. It was a deeply challenging time for Wendi and me. Diana and Keith were our support system. We were so grateful for them then, and now as I look back, I realize they looked after Phillip and George a lot while we were consumed with doctors and trying to find answers. We were both a mess emotionally. It is heartbreaking to see your child hooked up to intravenous tubes with a look on their face like "You are supposed to fix this; you're supposed to kiss the boo-boo and make it go away." As a parent, you are in an unfamiliar place. You are not sleeping well; you are probably in a bit of shock. You must balance all of that with making important decisions and being strong for your child. Not knowing what to expect does not make it easier. We learned that our little boys' temperaments were directly a reflection of Wendi and me. So, we had to try and be positive in front of him. I had heard that babies, when they are sick, go quickly, and I took that to heart. I did not verify if this was true or not. This was forty years ago, and access to medical information was not just a click away. I immediately became fearful for our baby and myself. While Wendi was off consulting with doctors, I went into the chapel at Long Island College Hospital and started praying. My prayer was this: If you, God, help my son to get well, I will leave the life of everyday drugs behind me again, and I will seek to know you in a deep and more meaningful way.

CHAPTER 7

Grateful to Be Alive

OUR BABY GOT WELL and came home from the hospital. We realized that it could have been much worse. Every time we saw our little boy's face, it was a reminder of how grateful we were and how our prayers had been answered. When I told them what had happened, some people may have thought that we were just lucky. Yes—in our minds, we might have thought that ourselves, but in our hearts, we knew better.

I have heard that a grateful attitude is one of the most effective ways to open the door to God. That has got to be true, because I felt that God was drawing me close to him. I was a washing machine full of feelings and emotions just whirling around—trying not to go into a spin cycle, just hoping for some stability, not sure that I could live the life that I had promised in my prayer. Then, something happened. Around the corner from where we lived, there was a church called The Brooklyn Tabernacle that was meeting in a onetime movie theater. It was (and still is) an evangelical, nondenominational church pastored by Jim Cymbala. The church was known for their Grammy Award winning choir. There was a poster in front of their building advertising that Dion would be there to share his faith and his music. I did not know that he had just released a new album called *Inside Job*. It was his first album of gospel songs he had written himself. The first chance I had, I made sure I went out and bought it.

I listened to it over and over till I could play every song on the guitar. Looking back, I can see that God doesn't have to wait for you to walk through the doors of a church to move in your life. Two songs absolutely grabbed a hold of me. The first was Dion's "The Truth Will Set You Free."

I found the words to be so heartful that I identified with him even more than I ever had. He was coming from a place of experiences that I had just left, it seemed like, the day before. Memories can be a pathway to success, or they can be a scar that disables you. Unless your life depends on it, change is never easy. Surrendering to change is not about running from something but running to something new and exciting. "Sweet Surrender" was another song that grabbed me.

I think the words of that song ring true in a lot of people, not just me. "I feel God tugging at me. I am still not sure I can do this," I was thinking. I kept thinking in terms of "I must change by my own strength and resist temptation." I had been disappointed so many times by someone trying to sell me something that was an empty promise. I had met the snake-oil salesman who had a cure-all for me, a seedy professional with a quick remedy. In the past, if I sensed that I was being tricked, I would hustle myself out the door like a groom late for a wedding. I was prepared to do that again if I had to.

The night I had been waiting for came. I was about to walk through the doors of The Brooklyn Tabernacle, which was a couple of steps from my front door. I started to recall the many times I had seen Dion live. So many times, I had been at the Murray the K shows to the bitter end and at the Westbury Music Fair, and I had seen the debut of Dion's *Return of the Wanderer* at the Bottom Line. But that was all showbiz—I was hoping this was going to be different. Dion was already sitting on the stage with Pastor Jim Cymbala and several other people when I got to my seat and sat down. There was a short introduction explaining how the night was going to flow, and then Pastor Jim started to preach before he introduced Dion. As I looked around, I felt intimidated by what I saw there. People were taking sermon notes and highlighting their bibles, and to me they looked like they were professionals at what they were doing. I did not know this was what people did in these services; I never saw that during Mass.

Dion was introduced and started to sing and share his faith when suddenly, the atmosphere changed—it was tangible, a feeling you could touch. This was not showbiz; this was genuine, sincere, and free from pretense, and what he shared was real. I started to see things in a different light. Could it be that the God of my youth was not mad at me at all—that I had value, that I was valuable to him? Could God really solve my problems and help me resolve my many issues? Church on Sunday is one thing, but what about the rest of the week?

Anyone could see that Dion had empathy and compassion for guys like me who had issues with fear, guilt, and shame. He related to feelings of being stuck in a place where you would take two steps forward and then take three steps back. The great thing was that he revisited all those emotions, and he got excited when he started talking about the hope that we find when we coexist alongside God, because we were created by God to work at maximum capacity when we are in union with him. To know God is to be fully alive as a human being, he would say.

Repentance is not the end but the beginning. Once you've experienced God for yourself, no one will be able to change your mind about him. To humble ourselves is to experience God, because he finds it irresistible when you seek his help. There is no life without this hunger.

CHAPTER 8

Finally, Freedom

IN THE SUMMER OF 1982,we moved to a different area of Brooklyn called Kensington. Wherever you might move to, it is good to be mindful that any move could either be an inconvenience or an opportunity to clean out the attic and get rid of those old, dusty magazines and those ancient souvenirs. I had an expectation that this move was going to be beneficial for us. I was making room for new friends, new memories, and new experiences. To learn how to be a better husband and a better father, and to be true to the prayer I had prayed a few months earlier, which—I believe—resulted in my youngest son getting well.

Our new place was twice the size as our apartment in Park Slope. The boys had a lot more room to play in and not be on top of each other, and Wendi and I had a little bit more privacy to enjoy ourselves together. The Kensington area of Brooklyn was full of tree-lined streets where kids played sports and had fun, like kids should. Not long after we moved there, George and Phillip were invited by Jim and John, who lived up the street, to what they called "Bible baseball" on a Friday night, a particularly useful and fun way to interact with the Bible and what it says. It involved a board game shaped like a baseball diamond; the objective was to get the questions right so you could get closer to home base.

I was excited when I was hired by the top supermarket chain on the East Coast. Great salary and benefits, a good pension—the only drawback was that I had to work the night shift. I was very willing to get my foot in the door, but after a year and a half, I was a mess. I didn't have unbroken sleep because of interruptions of a phone ringing or someone knocking on the door. I did all that I could do on the job to get an early shift—working extremely hard, talking with the higher-ups to get put on a day shift—but it was to no avail. One day, I yelled out to God, "I need your help," then I lay down and went to sleep.

Later in the day, Wendi came into the bedroom to wake me up to say I had a phone call from the district supervisor. The message he had for me was that I was being transferred to another store closer to home and would have a new schedule, working 8:00 a.m. to 5:00 p.m. I was ecstatic, because working a night shift had limited me from participating in many family outings. One was the neighborhood Missionary Alliance Church that met in the pastor's home. This was the same place my boys were going to for Bible baseball on Friday nights. Wendi and the boys got to know everyone well, but I had still not met them yet. Sunday came and there I was, meeting all these churchgoers that she had told me about. The genuine warmth they showed me was the equivalent of that showed to a long-lost son who had just come home.

I do not remember the sermon, but I recall the impression it had on me. The pastor was genuine—the real thing. He spoke with conviction but was gentle, not shouting to convey his point. I had been to enough ball games and had watched the loudest screamers leave halfway in the middle of the game. At church, I witnessed an inner strength that I did not have but wanted so badly. Pastor George grew up in a small town in Elysburg, Pennsylvania. Back then, it was a town of four hundred people. He wrestled in high school and became known as a jock/athlete. He never planned on going to college until his pastor pushed him to and helped him get accepted into Nyack College in New York. This is where he met Judy. In time, they fell in love and, after a while, got married. Judy Taylor was born into a missionary family and spent most of her childhood in Vietnam. After pastoring a couple of churches in New York State, Pastor George felt he had a calling on his life to go to New York City. Judy cried for a while, but thanks to her husband's perseverance and patience and a lot of prayer, God changed her heart so that she was willing to go.

She told me that after they moved to Kensington, Brooklyn, she stood on the corner waiting for the bus and thought, "I love Brooklyn." There was an innocence about them—they were not naive, but they were also not hard-edge, which is a by-product of living in the city.

Through George and Judy's example, I sensed that something was about to change in me, from seeking to finding the Maker of all that is to knowing him personally. Pastor George and Judy cared so much about me and my family, which reached me to the core. I learned through them that it is crucial to recognize God's acceptance if I am going to experience freedom from any addiction. God has seen it all, yet instead of drawing away in disgust, he draws closer. I had experienced withdrawal from heroin three times and withdrawal from methadone twice, so I knew what to expect. I was preparing for a battle. I even planned to be around Pastor George for the first three days. I wanted a long-term, sustained change, not a short-term improvement that would sputter out before real change happened. I did not want another gym membership that exploded in January and fizzled out in April.

Then, early one morning, I woke up, still half asleep, and I felt there was a presence all around me, like I had felt in the jail cell in the Brooklyn House of Detention on Atlantic Avenue. I felt truly alone, and I was on my knees, saying, "God, if you are real, I need your help." He was there in that cell then, and he was there when I woke up that morning, saying to me, "This is the day; I am here with you. Lean on me." One of the first things I would do in the morning was to drink a bottle of methadone and get ready for work, but I did not do that this morning. I left it alone. I worked all day and when I got home, I waited until after dinner and the boys had gone to bed, then I called Wendi to the kitchen sink. With my six bottles of methadone in my hands, I told her what had happened when I woke up and then proceeded to pour out the bottles into the sink.

Wendi's eyes were so big when I continued pouring the liquid into the sink. She said, "Maybe you should hold on to one bottle in case you get sick." After a couple of seconds, I responded, "No! This is real this time. I am not doing it alone."

The next couple of weeks were difficult. There were times I felt the temptation to take something or drink something. But the difference was that this time, I was not relying on my own strength. I kept thinking about how fortunate I was because our youngest son did not need to be in the hospital anymore and because of the loving family I now had. They were committed to me, and I was to them. People with whom I shared my experience would ask me how long it had been since I last did drugs, and I would simply say that it felt like years. When you realize that something supernatural has taken place, there is no such thing as time and space.

As the weeks went by, I made it a point to stay close to Pastor George, knowing that I would need prayer more than ever to make sure I would see this to the other side. The "Big Book" of Alcoholics Anonymous says you need a sponsor to walk with you in your recovery; Pastor George was mine. We grew to like and laugh with each other, and we would run into each other in the neighborhood all the time.

One such time was in the local grocery store that sold lottery tickets. There was one line specifically for people who were buying lottery tickets. While standing in the line that sold lottery tickets, I noticed that Pastor George was standing a few people in front of me. I thought to myself, "Shouldn't he have more faith in God to supply all his needs?" This was followed by another thought: "What about me?"

It turned out that when Pastor George got to the front with groceries in his arms, he found out he was in the wrong line. He should had been in the line to buy groceries, not lottery tickets. Was this a coincidence that I was in the grocery store at that precise time to witness this? I immediately started to feel shame for thinking what I had thought and went home and wrote this song:

> I don't need any Horoscope or Fortune
> Telling cards to help me cope
> With the pressures and strides of my life
> And I don't need any fancy cars
> A house on a hill or a pool in the yard
> To give me the peace that you placed
> In my heart, I just need you . . .
> Seeing a man dressed in colored tights
> Throwing a ball to some new heights
> Can't excite me the way your words do
> Or standing in some lottery line, a drug store
> Or liquor store line, won't do for me
> What you can do, I just need you
> Only you can satisfy our lives . . .
> And I don't need any stocks and bonds
> Or some drug dealer to turn me on to a
> Fortune that's made destroying people's lives
> 'Cause my treasure lies in my eternal life
> And my relationship with Jesus Christ
> He is the lord of my life
> I just need you, only you can satisfy
> Our lives.

CHAPTER 9

Engagement on East Fourth Street

AT LAST, SPRING HAD arrived and any last remnants of winter were gone. The neighborhood seemed like it was just waiting to come alive. We all had more reasons to be outside instead of indoors hibernating. For me, it was much more than that the sun was out and nature was starting to bloom—I was beginning to feel a part of it all. No longer on the fringe of society, my lone-wolf days were far behind me now. I shared common attitudes and interest in the community.

Wendi and the boys were beginning to have real friendships with the people that lived on our street and at the church. I still had issues with trust, but I was slowly coming around. Jim and Ida made it easy for me to relax and not be defensive when I was wrong about something—having to be right all the time is a tough way to live. You find yourself always defending or protecting a position when it is so much easier to say you were wrong or you made a mistake. Sometimes you get tangled up with the small things when a simple "I am sorry; I was wrong" will satisfy.

Wendi and I began to go out for coffee a lot with Jim and Ida— since we sat beside them in church every Sunday, it was inevitable. We were only a couple years younger than they were, so it was easy for us to look to them as spiritual parents, because they knew so much more about the apologetics of our faith. As we got to know each other and each other's families, we realized that the apartments that we were living in and renting had no backyard for our families to have barbecues and parties outside. With rents increasing, we decided that together we would be able to qualify for a mortgage. At that time in Brooklyn, you needed at least $50,000 to even be considered by a real-estate company and for them to take you seriously and take you to see a home.

We quickly found out that two family homes were way out of our price range. One of the blessings of having a friend like Jim was that he had already owned homes out of state and had an ability when it came to finances and numbers to be creative and think outside the box. One such suggestion was that we consider renting with an option to buy. Even though it was such a long shot in Brooklyn, we did find a house.

There was a lady that owned a home on the same street that Wendi and I lived on, and it was empty and available. Jim, being a skilled negotiator, made her an offer she could not refuse. We offered to pay back all mortgage payments that were delinquent plus a few thousand dollars as a down payment. We decided that Wendi and I would live on the first two floors and Jim and Ida and their family would live on the top two floors. Our families grew closer together as well as our church family at Christ Community.

After we were in the house for a few months, an opportunity came up to have church in our home. A dispute came up with the city on the size of the church meeting. So, Jim, with some help from his sons, knocked down a wall to make a bigger room so we could gather at our new place. It has been said that "what you feed grows, and what you starve will die." Having church in our home was an avenue to feed our faith. Yes, we had basic faith to believe there is a God, but we needed to build our faith for the daily testing life brings to us. Faith is not separate from reason—it is the continuance of it.

Another year had gone by when I got a visit from a musician friend of mine, with whom—only a handful of years earlier—I had been shooting dope when I overdosed. I had woken up in a shower fully clothed, with him slapping my face till I came back, never once thinking about my family and the heartache and grief they would experience seeing me on a slab in the morgue. So, there I was, standing beside the same friend who had prevented me from death, who was telling me that because he had continued using drugs long after I'd left that scene, he was HIV positive and was dying of AIDS. Less than a year later, he was gone, leaving behind a wife and two baby girls. It was tragic the number of friends that died because of AIDS during that time. I remembered that I had shared my faith when I was with him last, and knowing that words spoken in love and understanding are never wasted, I felt relieved that he was at peace.

I started settling into genuine family life, community life, and relationships that only required honesty and virtues like integrity and truthfulness. I'd left these virtues behind in my drug-induced coma days, but I was starting to get them all back.

The Kensington neighborhood has many Orthodox Jewish families that were priced out of Borough Park, a vibrant Jewish community. The Jewish center was a communal anchor, addressing the many local elderly Holocaust survivors. Wikipedia notes that "according to halakah, the operation of a motor vehicle constitutes multiple violations of the prohibited activities on Shabbat (the Jewish Sabbath)."[1] Besides this, "the law of techum shabbat limits on the distance one may travel beyond the city/town where one is spending Shabbat, regardless of the method of transportation. . . . Orthodox Judaism frowns upon those who purchase a home too far to walk to a synagogue."[2]

So, in retrospect, it should not have been a surprise when the new rabbi at the Jewish center came knocking on our door, asking to buy our house. The house was only two blocks walking distance from the Jewish synagogue. What makes this interesting is that

1. Wikipedia, s.v. "Driving on Shabbat," https://en.wikipedia.org/wiki/Driving_on_Shabbat.

2. Wikipedia, s.v. "Driving on Shabbat," https://en.wikipedia.org/wiki/Driving_on_Shabbat.

we did not own the home but had a legal document stating that if we could not get a mortgage from a bank, we had an option to sell our house. We tried to get Fannie Mae to agree to a thirty-year mortgage, but we were turned down. We agreed to sell the house and started looking for a place to move to, but the prospects were not so encouraging. We had to consider new school districts and neighborhoods that welcomed diverse families. The results were that we found nothing that suited our needs. I remember the day we were driving along Sixteenth Avenue in Borough Park heading home, discussing a place where we could live, when Wendi asked, "What about moving to Florida?" We were all in the car heading north to Kensington when she said "Florida," and I had to control myself so as not to make a U-turn and start heading south to Florida. I'd had a secret desire ever since that first trip in July of 1980 to live in Florida—now, six years later, it was an extraordinarily strong possibility.

I took some vacation time, and we all went to Florida to evaluate if we could begin a new life there. We were only there for a week, and everything fell into place: a new job, a place to live, family all around us—life was good. On the plane ride back to Brooklyn, I had a thought: Did this all simply happen? Was this just a coincidence? My secret desire to move to Florida was coming to pass, and the selling of a house we did not own was just unheard of. Albert Einstein, the theoretical physicist who developed the theory of relativity, is commonly credited with saying that "coincidence is God's way of remaining anonymous."[3]

3. Einstein, "Coincidence is God's . . ."

CHAPTER 10

Gratitude in Action

WHEN WE ARRIVED IN Florida, I felt as if I had broken free from the past, not only physically but also emotionally. I was in paradise now—everywhere I looked, it seemed that way. Palm trees everywhere; the smell of the ocean water; hundreds of miles of white, sandy beaches; and birds singing. I went walking along Las Olas Boulevard in Fort Lauderdale filming, and as I walked down the beach with my camera, I was thinking to myself, "This is truly a nirvana moment—I have found my Shangri-La."

Our new home was on a half acre of land with a built-in swimming pool in a quiet neighborhood. Wendi stayed at home with the boys while I worked at my new job. All we needed now was to find a church where we could feel accepted and grow in spiritual things. After a few Sunday-morning worship services at different churches, we found the one for us. There were no probing questions about our intentions or hints that it was time for us to join and get busy. None of that—just a sincere belief that "God loves you and wants to bless you." They wanted us to know that God said, "For I know the plans I have for you . . . plans to prosper you and not to harm you, plans to give you hope and a future (Jer 29:11).

We got there when the church was beginning to grow in number each week. The excitement and anticipation were contagious—you could feel it a mile away. Before, we had been involved in a church with a couple dozen people, and now we were in a house of faith that had a few thousand. I credit Wendi's countenance and genuine friendliness as opening the door to finding favor. When she smiled, people would gravitate toward her. Standing beside her made it easy for the heads of different ministries to get to know me. Eventually, Wendi got involved with the nursery. That was not the place for me, because if I held a baby in my arms, it would start to cry, and if the baby were not crying, then you knew it was a doll. I was not a natural. The prison ministry was more of my calling, and with my guitar and story songs of prison and drugs, the inmates were very attentive. I knew from my own experience that there were men who were there because of the parole board and that it would look good for them to try to rehabilitate themselves. But then there were men who were broken and open to change; personally, I knew only too well the two sides of that coin.

As I began to have more of an understanding of how addictions occur, I was asked by an associate pastor named Eric to start a recovery group for people who were addicted to drugs or alcohol. One of the many that came to these meetings was Sam, who had a real desire to be free of drugs and alcohol after many years of addiction. He was very new at this, especially in his newfound faith and living it. Once, I got a call late at night from him. He asked me if I would come quickly to the emergency room at a local hospital, because his mother was dying.

He was in his early forties, as I was, so I could relate to him—his emotions and uncertainty about the future. His mom was lying there in a coma in the emergency room. With great sorrow and weeping, Sam asked me if I would pray that God would assure him that he would see his mom again. He was uncertain of her beliefs. Sam thought his mother was a Christian, but he needed some last-minute proof.

While our hands were resting on her, I prayed an amazingly simple prayer that God would reveal to Sam what he was hoping to know—that he would see her again. A minute or two later, his mom sat up on the gurney, still in a coma, and said, "There is but one God, one Holy Spirit, and one Jesus Christ." After saying that, she lay back down, still in a coma, and passed away an hour or so later. It always amazes me the extent God will go to in order to draw you close to him and to always validate to you that you are on the right path to knowing him. It is an expression of love and acceptance from him to you.

I have found that you can convey a feeling of love in a four-minute song when it might take a motivational speaker or preacher an hour to penetrate the most calloused heart. I get great joy from taking people on a journey with a song, and over the next couple of years, I had many opportunities to do just that. Pastor Rick and Pastor Kathy Thomas were very instrumental in making that happen. Pastor Rick was hosting on Trinity Broadcasting Network (TBN), and Pastor Kathy was the director of music. Their kindness opened a lot of doors for me. They were always incredibly supportive, along with Pastor Eric. With the release of my first album, *I Just Need You*, there were several guest appearances on TBN, followed by a feature newspaper story.

Our friends from Brooklyn, Jim and Ida, did not get TBN in New York at that time and asked if I could send them recordings of the shows. With much procrastination, I finally sent them a few shows. I do not remember why there was a delay in me getting the videos to them, but when they finally got them, their equipment to play the videos did not work. So they called a couple they had just met at the church in Brooklyn who lived a block away. They told them that they had been waiting for such a long time to see these shows and now could not. They asked if they could watch them together at their home. It was a perfect opportunity for fellowship with new people at their church. Jelly and Hank told them to come on over. Jelly and Hank's experiences living in Brooklyn were so much different from those of Jim and Ida. What they had in common was their faith. As they all sat there in the living room watching the opening of the program with me singing a song, Hank looked at everyone with surprise and, somewhat startled, said, "I know him, that's Eddy Mastellone. Gee, I thought he was dead from a bullet or a drug overdose."

What is so amazing about this is that just a week earlier, Hank had gone forward to make a commitment to receive Christ and to live his life through him. As he had stood there, this big, muscular man had said to the pastor in a genuine, emotional voice, "I am not sure God can fix me, let alone change my life. He does not know what I have done or where I have been. You people are all nice and caring. I was raised on the streets with the gangs, the drugs, the women. I have not had a holy or a pleasant life." So a group of ministers had prayed for him, asking that God would send the perfect witness to him, someone Hank could not deny was changed who would validate the truth that he could change his life if only he would let God.

It always amazes me the extent to which God will go to draw you close to him and how he will always validate you and show you that you are on the right path to knowing him. It is his expression of love and acceptance from him to you.

Island of Martinique

The Mastellone Family, 1948

Eddy at Six Years Old

Grandma and Grandpa Mastellone

Mastellone Family, 1910

Brownsville Projects, 1958

Inner City Brooklyn

Inmate Bible Study, Dannamora, New York, 1977

Phillp and George,
Grandarmy Plaza, Brooklyn

Saint Augustine,
Parkslope, Brooklyn

Our Family and Our Extended Family   **Jim and Ida**

Wendi and Eddy

Pastor George and Judy

East 4 Street, Brooklyn

Bushkill Falls, New York

East 4 Street, Our First Big Snow Storm

My First Album

First Christmas in Our New Home

Tropicana Dinner Theater

Eddy and Hank

■ SUN-SENTINEL ■ SUNDAY, DECEMBER 29, 1991

CONVERT WITH CONVICTION

Former convict Ed Mastellone sings songs of hope and love at the Abundant Life Christian Center.

Page 11

1. YOU NEED A LOVE
2. 7TH AVE
3. SOME THINGS STILL REMAIN THE SAME
4. CHANGE OUR LIVES, LORD
5. SURRENDER
6. I'M SO FREE
7. GONNA MAKE A DIFFERENCE
8. LITTLE ONE
9. THE TRUTH IS
10. COME AND DANCE WITH ME

© ℗ 2003 EDDY MASTELLONE
www.eddy49.com

New York City-born and raised, the streets, the neighborhood, the challenge, his journey: Much of it Eddy expresses in these songs. The battle, the grace, the splendor of truth, the fight and the victory . . . *"All are Living Proof."*
— Dion

Living Proof Album

Chapter 11

The Past Catches Up

During the fall of 1995, I went for my annual physical with my primary care doctor. He was alarmed at what he found in my blood work; he did not tell me anything more except to say he was sending me to a specialist. I made an appointment to see Dr. Ross. The nurse called back saying the doctor wanted to see my wife and I together, because it was especially important. We were very anxious, to say the least. You try not to think the worst or of all the what-ifs, but catastrophic fantasies cause useless suffering in our minds, whether there is a grain of truth to them or not. As Mark Twain allegedly said, "I am an old man and have known a great many troubles, but most of them never happened."[1]

The doctor informed us that I had been diagnosed with the virus hepatitis C. He also said that there was a treatment plan that was experimental, and that Dr. Ross would get me on the plan, because the drugs involved would be very costly. Hepatitis C is a serious liver disease caused by the hepatitis C virus. The most common way to get hepatitis C is by encountering the blood of someone who has it. You can live for years without feeling sick, but the virus can still damage your liver, even when there are not any symptoms. You

1. Twain, "I am an old . . ."

could also spread the virus to others without knowing it. A blood test would be the way to know if you are positive.

Before 1992, there was no test to screen the blood for hepatitis C. The virus spread through exposure to blood and blood products such as transfusions, exposure to contaminated needles, and organ transplants. Life-threatening complications such as liver cancer and liver failure from hepatitis C are on the rise, as people who do not know they have hepatitis C go undiagnosed.[2]

According to Dr. Melissa Carroll with Healthline.com, "In 1995, scientists discovered that if you mixed the injectable IFNa with the antiviral drug ribavirin (RBV), results improved."[3] These drugs do not target the virus that made you sick—instead, they amp up your immune system so you can fight it the way you do when you get the flu. People who stuck with the yearlong treatment—not all did—had to live with chemo-like side effects.

After hearing the news, we did not panic—keep in mind this was all very new in the medical field—and we assured each other we would handle it together. We had to consider to what extent I should be quarantined from the family to avoid possible blood exposure—shaving, razor cuts, etc. The hard part was the constant fatigue and loss of appetite. My job was sales, and being in a management position, I could not afford to look lazy or unproductive. The very last thing I wanted were interactions with customers. After a little less than a year, the doctor had me stop, because I was suffering from anemia. A month later, he had me begin again. This went on for another six months until it happened again.

I was suffering from a low red-blood-cell count; every month, Dr. Ross would have my blood checked. In the meantime, I learned about healing and the scriptures pertaining to healing: "Heal me, Lord, and I will be healed; save me and I will be saved, for you are the one I praise" (Jer 17:14). I had many men and women of faith pray and lay hands on me. I have seen people instantly healed the moment they were prayed for—that is not how it happened for me. Dr. Ross was able to have me start on the medicine again, but before

2. Centers for Disease Control and Prevention, "Viral Hepatitis."

3 Carroll, "Then and Now," para. 8.

he did, he had me take another blood test; that was on Tuesday morning. The next day, I went to a midweek church service. I sat in the back and during the service, I heard that small, still voice say, "I have healed you, now go tell someone." Two days later, I got a call from Dr. Ross telling me he was stopping all treatment, because my blood-test results showed no sign of the virus hepatitis C.

A couple of years had gone by from start to finish, and in all that time, I could not grasp that hepatitis C would be the end of me. The message I'd heard at every church service for eight years was that God loves me. By the time I was diagnosed, it was ingrained into my DNA that God genuinely loves me. He took me out of a lifestyle that caused many people I knew to die because of drug overdose or AIDS. I just could not believe that God would let me die from the side effects so many years later. Sometimes, what we thought was the end turns out to be the beginning.

I have learned that God looks beyond your needs to how your life will effect the people with whom you come into contact. A few hundred thousand people die worldwide from hepatitis C every year. If one day there is a cure for the virus, it still does not negate what he did for you.

Chapter 12

"Ancient Voices"

WELL, AFTER HAVING A medical problem that could have resulted in death, I wanted to search deeper into my faith. I was ready for all the tragedies and all the victories of trying to live a life of faith. Someone once said to me that the Bible is not a fairy tale that took place in a far-off, unreal place with unreal people. Instead, it took place in real time, with real people, in a real place.

A by-product of growing up in New York City culture for me was being suspicious of everyone. Everyone had a secret agenda, and there was a conspiracy behind everything. Now, of course, over the many years of growing in my faith, I toned this attitude of pessimism down quite a lot. But it was still there like it was in my DNA. So when an opportunity came up for me to see the Holy Land with a couple dozen pastors from all over the United States and to see with my own eyes where the events I had been reading about had happened, I jumped right on it.

It was a few months after the Twin Towers were destroyed, and a few of my friends were concerned that I might be going into a war zone. Nine hundred million people live, work, and play in Israel, where security is paramount. This is a country that knows how to deal with challenges quickly and efficiently. The group I was going with was made up of pastors with their wives who were coming from as far away as Alaska and California, so we all met at the Toronto Pearson International Airport Terminal 1 for Air Canada. We arrived in Tel Aviv twelve hours later, landing at Ben Gurion AirPort. As I left the plane to walk along the tarmac to the terminal, the moment my feet touched the ground, something happened inside of me. It did not make a bit of sense. I had a strong feeling like every cell in my body was being illuminated. During my twelve hours on the plane, I hadn't reflected on what I would feel like once our plane had arrived. I was tired and wanted to take a shower and go to sleep. If it were Naples, Italy, where my bloodline was from, that would make sense, but this did not. I was feeling teary-eyed and overwhelmed with the feeling that I was home.

On the way to the Ramat Rachel Hotel in Jerusalem, where we would be staying for the next couple of days, this experience on the tarmac weighed heavily on my mind. Was I really home? In the morning, we began our day of touring at the Mount of Olives and then descended to the Garden of Gethsemane. Ancient olive trees still stand there, some more than two thousand years old. There is a church there that is called the Church of All Nations, also known as the Basilica of the Agony. It enshrines a section of bedrock where Jesus is said to have prayed before his arrest. Next, we visited the House of Caiaphas, where Jesus was held the night before his crucifixion. Later, we visited the Upper Room, where we had a time of worship and devotion.

My personal experience in the Upper Room was that everyone there wanted a manifestation of the Lord amongst the gathering. I have learned through the years how important expectations are when you want a real, tangible presence of the Lord. Humbling yourself is also paramount for that experience to happen. While kneeling, God reminded me of all the places I have felt his presence because I was desperate to know him.

∽

Later that day, we visited the Church of the Nativity and Shepherds' Field in Bethlehem. There was so much to take in and so many emotions to process. Before we headed back to the hotel in Jerusalem, we took a much-needed break at a roadside café. I sat at a table outside, just about a half mile from the Church of the Nativity, watching a lamb hide from its shepherd. The rest of the herd was in the field, but this lone lamb decided to run off. Across the road from me was a garbage dumpster that the little lamb was using to evade the shepherd. The shepherd was dressed in the traditional garments that shepherds have worn for the last few thousand years. What struck me was that neither one of them could the see the other, but they still knew they were a few feet apart. I was close enough to hear if the shepherd was calling the lamb, but he was not. It led me to believe that the lamb sensed the shepherd nearby. The shepherd suddenly did a quick maneuver and scooped up the baby lamb and brought it back to the herd. It gave me great delight to watch this whole thing take place in less than five minutes. It reminded me that sheep were the first creatures to witness a sky filled with angels as their shepherds heard the good news of Jesus's birth. God could have sent the news of the newborn King to the palace or the temple. Instead, he announced the arrival of the Lamb to a field full of sheep. Jesus is often compared to a lamb because he was meek and nonthreatening. Even in heaven when the day of the Lord arrives, Jesus is still called the Lamb (Rev 5:13).

God's people are compared to sheep for several reasons. One reason is that sheep are one of the few animals that do not have a defense system. Sheep are helpless without a shepherd. The first line of Ps 23:1 reflects this: "The Lord is my shepherd, I lack nothing." Another reason human beings are compared to sheep is that sheep are prone to wander away from the flock. A sheep's only chance of survival is with the flock under the care of a competent shepherd. Yet, they become overconfident, rebellious, or distracted and wander away.

~

One of Jesus's most known parables is about a lamb that strayed so far from the flock, it became lost. The Good Shepherd left the ninety-nine sheep in the field and went in search of the one lost sheep (Luke 15:3–7). I guess the reason why this event with the Shepherd touched me so deeply that I remembered it so many years later was that I felt like I was lost for so long, but then I was found by the Good Shepherd.

The next morning, we were on our way to Caesarea, Megiddo, and Tiberias. As we drove along the Mediterranean Sea to Caesarea, the water looked so inviting—I could not wait to take a swim. This ancient seaport was built by Herod the Great, and while I was walking around the amphitheater, what I thought were tiny rocks under my feet were pieces of broken pottery. I was walking on history. As I continued walking through the ruins, I found a place to sit and watch the waves crash along the walls of the aqueduct. This structure was built in the year 20 BC and supplied fresh, clean water for baths and fountains, and drinking water for ordinary citizens throughout the region.

Caesarea Philippi, as it was known back then, was a pagan city. Located some twenty-five miles north of the Sea of Galilee, the "water supply has made the area very fertile and attractive for religious worship. Numerous temples were built in this city in the Hellenistic and Roman periods."[1] One of these areas was a place at the foot of Mount Harmon, a place that had several buildings that were used in worshiping the Greek god Pan. A "spring emerged from the large cave which became the center of pagan worship," involving major orgies, sexual activities of all kinds, idolatry, etc. The Greek god Pan was half man and half goat and the god of fright, and "is often depicted playing the flute."[2]

As I was walking among the ruins, I could feel the hair on the back of my neck standing up. There was still a remnant of evil that resided there which was very tangible. Before I learned of the events that had taken place there, I felt a leftover residue of something very dark. You can find out a lot by reading the historian Josephus's writings and the Book of Enoch, an ancient Hebrew religious text on the origins of demons and giants that also explains why some angels fell from heaven. In that same text, it is

1. "Caesarea Philippi," para. 2.
2. "Caesarea Philippi," para. 5.

believed that Mount Harmon was the spot where the fallen angels first touched the earth when they were cast out of heaven.[3]

So when we read Matt 16:13–18, it all makes sense:

> When Jesus came to the region of Caesarea Philippi, he asked his disciples, "Who do people say the Son of Man is?"
>
> They replied, "Some say John the Baptist; others say Elijah; and still others, Jeremiah or one of the prophets."
>
> "But what about you?" he asked. "Who do you say I am?"
>
> Simon Peter answered, "You are the Messiah, the Son of the living God."
>
> Jesus replied, "Blessed are you, Simon son of Jonah, for this was not revealed to you by flesh and blood, but by my Father in heaven. And I tell you that you are Peter, and on this rock I will build my church, and the gates of Hades will not overcome it.

According to our guide, many Bible scholars believe that Jesus was standing in front of the twenty-foot-high gates that were the entrance to the cave where the worshiping of the Greek god Pan took place.

The afternoon was spent at Megiddo and the Valley of Armageddon, and then we were on our way to Nazareth, Cana, and Tiberius. We spent the next week near the Sea of Galilee at a kibbutz hotel. According to the Tourist Israel website, "Kibbutz hotels are a unique Israeli form of hospitality."[4] I stayed in a small villa on the property that was a couple hundred feet from the seashore. In the morning, I had breakfast and then boarded a motor launch for a cruise across the Sea of Galilee to Capernaum. After our visit to the ruins of the second-century synagogue, we preceded to Tabgha, the place of the multiplication of loaves and fishes. Next was the Mount of Beatitudes, where Jesus delivered the Sermon on the Mount. It was amazing to test the acoustics of the area—you could say something and it would be heard across the surrounding area.

---

3. Gilbert, "Mount Hermon."

4. "Best Kibbutz Hotels," para. 1.

We preceded to the Jordan River, where my experience was a time of great spiritual blessing never to be forgotten. To be baptized in the Jordan River at Yardenit Baptismal Site was one of the highlights of my visit to the Holy Land—to think that Jesus started his ministry after he was baptized by John the Baptist in the Jordan River. In Christianity, baptism is a sign of repentance and forgiveness of sins. Christians are baptized in the name of the Father, the Son, and the Holy Spirit. Through baptism, Christians associate with the death, burial, and resurrection of Jesus.

We returned to our compound on the Sea of Galilee. After dinner, I decided to walk down to the beach. By that time, it was late in the evening. It was dark out, and the light from the moon illuminated the small waves hitting the beach. It was so peaceful, even somewhat mystical, standing there by myself with no one around. I started recalling the many stories of Jesus on the sea with his disciples.

It was time to head back to the villa to get some sleep. During that night, I had nightmares about demonic spirits that were trying to harm me. These dreams were not the ordinary dreams I usually had. These were more like virtual reality dreams. I remembered having read the book by Watchman Nee called *Spiritual Authority.*[5] What I had learned from the book was to say, "Stop!" and take authority over them in Jesus's name. In the morning, I woke up with an inner peace all around me and thought, "People come and go. They live out their lives and then die, but evil spirits do not die. They can be sent into pigs and drown, as depicted in the story of Jesus casting out demons from a man who was possessed. The pigs die, but the demons do not. They still go on to cause havoc from generation to generation in people's lives . . ."

The next morning, we journeyed through the Jordan Valley to Jericho, the old Canaanite city destroyed by Joshua. It is the oldest-known inhabited city in the world. We saw excavations of Jericho, the mountains of Moab, Elisha's Fountain, and the Mount of Temptation. After a brief stop for lunch, we made our way to the Dead Sea, then on to Masada. We ascended to the top of Masada

5. Nee, *Spiritual Authority.*

by cable car to visit the ruins of the fortress where, in 70 AD, the Jewish defenders made their last stand in the First Jewish Revolt against Rome. Once we got to the top of Masada, we saw the remains of the storehouses, cisterns, and a sixth-century Byzantine church. The following morning, we followed the footsteps of Jesus back to Jerusalem. The Ramat Rachel Hotel welcomed us back for another four days. We got to take a walking tour of the old city of Jerusalem. The day started with a visit to Jaffa Gate and the Jewish Quarter, where we went into the marketplace to buy memorable things to bring back home. I made a point to haggle over prices but never over tips.

A Jewish friend of mine whose father had passed away a month or so earlier asked me for a favor—that while I was at the "Wailing Wall" I would slip a prayer on paper with regard to his dad between the stones of the wall.

After leaving the wall, it was a short walk to Mount Moriah, which is called the Temple Mount. That is where Abraham's offering of Isaac as a sacrifice to God took place. After lunch, we saw the Church of St. Anne, a church built by the Crusaders, then the Pool of Bethesda and the remains of the Antonia Fortress, which is believed by tradition to be the site of the trial of Jesus. We then walked along the Via Dolorosa and left the Old City through the Damascus Gate. From there, we preceded to the Garden Tomb to celebrate Communion beside the empty tomb, which was truly a memorable time. After that, we headed back to the hotel for dinner and sleep.

The following day began with a drive through the Kidron Valley. We saw the tombs of Absalom, Zachariah, and James. Then, we drove to the Pool of Siloam, the Valley of Hinnom, and King Herod's family tomb. Afterward, we headed back once again to visit the Old City, where we saw Pilate's judgment Hall and the Chapel of the Flagellation. In the afternoon, we visited the outdoor Holyland Model of Jerusalem and then Yad Vashem, Israel's memorial to the six million Jews who perished during the Holocaust. You cannot leave that memorial without shedding a lot of tears. We left the memorial and went to Israel's parliament, the Knesset building, and learned a lot about current events while viewing the modern parts of Jerusalem.

So much history—the blood, the wars. Walking along the stone streets of the Old City exceeded all my expectations. Over three million people a year make this same pilgrimage, often in search of a new or expanded understanding of themselves, others, human nature, and a higher good. One of the events that impressed me was that when I was on my way to the "Wailing Wall," I had to move to the side of the walkway leading to the wall. We made way to let new recruits of the Israeli army, who had just turned eighteen years old, view all the historical places. Part of the army's strategy for the new recruits was to impress upon them the history of Israel through the historic sites, so that on the battlefield they would have the image fused into their memory and would fight harder. This event that took place with the new recruits at the "Wailing Wall" was the essence of why I went to Israel. To know and feel what I was fighting for, and to know my moral and spiritual significance.

CHAPTER 13

Cadillacs End Up in the Junkyard

FLYING BACK ON THE plane, I had a lot of time to think about where I had just been. The places, the people, the friends I had made, and the spiritual insight I had gained. While I was reliving the experience, I felt that God was reminding me about something—that as a teenager, I had participated in alienating different ethnic groups from myself. Well, the revelation I got was that I was doing the same thing with the church. I was finding fault with every church except the one I was in. I once heard someone say that if you find the perfect church, you better leave, because you'll ruin it. I know God does not blame me for being an individual but rather for my individualism. God's greatest problem is not the outward divisions and denominations that divide his church but our own individualistic hearts. I figured out that I could analyze along with the best of them why this church does things right and that church does things wrong, but when God measures a man, he puts the tape around his heart, not his head.

Before I'd left for Israel, my youngest son, Michael, had gone to a young adults' meeting at a church in Boca Raton, Florida. There, to his surprise, he met Dion and his wife, Susan, who were there to encourage the young adults in their faith. He found out that Dion would be speaking at a men's event in a few weeks, and Dion challenged the young adults to tell their fathers about it.

During that time, there was a lot of negative news in the newspapers and on TV about abuses of the church clergy. I wrote Dion a very personal letter asking him not to back out of this big event because of these church scandals. I wrote to him about his music and how it had gotten me through each rough phase in my life, especially his faith. I told him that men needed to hear what he had to say. A couple of weeks went by after I got back from Israel, and then we went to this motivational men's event. Dion was there, and he did not disappoint. He had a message for the men that was not only challenging but uplifting and truly relevant. Michael ran into him again at another meeting in Boca Raton. He knew I was Michael's father from the letter I had sent him and asked about me and wanted to meet me. We met for lunch at a diner in Boca Raton. As we sat there—just the two of us having lunch—Dion laid out the ground rules for our conversations. He knew that I was a longtime fan and wanted to set the perimeters. We would not be discussing music unless he brought it up. He wanted two people who loved the Lord and would enrich each other's lives, not a fan idolizing a rock and roll Hall of Famer. Was this another one of those coincidences that happens in life, or was God up to something?

Three years later, I was getting ready to introduce Dion, who was the special guest speaker at a spiritually based event. I knew there would be an excessively big crowd and that they would expect him to sing, like he did the last time he was at this event. Unfortunately, that was not going to happen, because he had a cold. He would have canceled but did not want to disappoint the men who were coming to hear him. So I had the people in the media room cue up a DVD of him singing "Amazing Grace" a cappella, which was so unique and soulful. As the DVD finished, I began to quote phrases from Lou Reed, Bruce Springsteen, and Bob Dylan about Dion and how much he had influenced their music. After I finished, Dion came up on stage and said, "Eddy and I go out to lunch a lot. Eddy talks about the diet he is on. We talk about sizes and shapes, and then we get a couple of sides of meatballs and bread. We are incredibly good talkers."

Sitting there in the front row listening to Dion, I reflected for a moment on a time some twenty years earlier when I was in the Brooklyn Tabernacle on Flatbush Avenue, listening to him share his faith and sing songs from his album *Inside Job*. This building was only a mile from the Fox Theatre, where I had seen him so many times at Murray the K's rock and roll shows, where Dion would be performing his number one hit for that year. I was sitting there surrounded by a couple thousand people, and none of them knew my name. But it did not matter, because there is a God in heaven who knows my name, and I was hoping that these men at this meeting would leave knowing the same thing I had felt twenty years earlier.

A few months later, Dion got tickets for an Emmylou Harris concert in West Palm Beach and invited me to come along. I was driving Wendi's new Ford Windstar van. Dion sat beside me in the passenger seat, giving me directions to the theater where the concert was. Susan, his wife, was behind us with a friend. Wendi had a prior commitment and could not be with us. There is a lot of music history that surrounds Emmylou Harris. A lot of people know her from the collaboration she did with Dolly Parton and Linda Ronstadt called *Trio* that sold four million copies. She has won fourteen Grammys, including induction into the Country Music Hall of Fame.

We got there and took our seats in the middle of the second row. Emmylou Harris took the stage, looking and singing like an angel with a white, ankle-length dress and platinum hair. Sitting five feet from where she stood, I could not help but think how precious she was. Dion had arranged for us to meet Emmylou after the concert. We were escorted to a staircase that took us to an apartment on the top floor of the theater. After Dion introduced us to Emmylou, she immediately went into telling us about a concert that she had been at some thirty years earlier. At this concert, Dion, Gram Parsons, and some friends of theirs had sung and harmonized to Dion's song "Abraham, Martin and John," and there had been something spiritual that was going on while they sang that she would never forget. Dion told me later that moments like that are incredibly special and almost impossible to recreate.

The year was 2002 and we were in Boca Raton in a Thai restaurant. Dion and I were sitting looking over the menu. Being indecisive, we were asking each other, "What are you going to have?" We decided on the same item: cashew chicken over jasmine rice (that ended up being our favorite every time we went there). Somehow, we started our conversation that day talking about the news, our family, and faith. As we sat there eating our meal, Dion asked me how much I thought God was involved with Wendi entering my life. I answered that at the time, I had not been thinking along those lines, but now, looking back, he had been very involved. Not because we were righteous (maybe Wendi had been, but I had been far from having any attributes of God). Redemption is prior to righteousness. You cannot be righteous until you are first redeemed. After I answered Dion, he shared with me that men are always looking for a female that is a perfect "ten." He said we end up settling for a "five" or "six" when God wants us to have a soul mate that is perfection, but only what he considers a "ten." If you are fortunate enough to recognize that he brought that person into your life, be astounded by it. Be grateful. Treasure the gift. Failing to notice a gift dishonors it and the gift giver. While Dion was talking, my mind did a split screen in an instant. I recalled hearing Bill McCartney giving a motivational speech at a Promise Keepers event and saying, "You will know if you are a successful, loving husband by the countenance your wife is wearing."[1] However, I read the following about Bill in a *New York Times* article:

> Bill McCartney, then the celebrated coach of the University of Colorado football team, was busier than ever organizing Promise Keepers, the Christian men's movement he had founded, which was gearing up for its largest stadium revival rally yet.

1. It was at a Promise Keepers event in St. Petersburg, Florida, I believe around 1997.

> While Mr. McCartney was out building a movement whose central tenet is that men should treasure and serve their wives and families, his own wife now says, she was suffering through the most precarious days of a marriage that has now lasted 35 years. . . .
>
> A private person, Mrs. McCartney until now has never talked publicly about her own feelings of marital despair and isolation that she grappled with even after her husband had begun drawing tens of thousands of men to stadium rallies with the message that they must make a new and passionate commitment to their wives and families.[2]

Lyndi said of her husband in a loving way that for a while, he was the "same as a plumber . . . A plumber never fixes anything at home . . . He's always out fixing everybody else's plumbing."[3]

A person's countenance can draw you to them when they have a vibe about them that is exciting, joyful, and very genuine. The thought that my actions and lack of appreciation could affect my wife's appearance broke my heart.

Back to Dion. He continued by saying, "Eve was not Adam's idea; Eve was God's idea. If it were not for God, Adam would have never realized that it was not good for him to be alone. He did not know any better. He was not lonely—walking with God, you are never lonely. Adam did not design Eve's feminine heart or female body; Adam did not do anything. He was fast asleep when God handcrafted her to help him. So be grateful for what you have. Love is not a feeling—it is a choice; it is a decision. You choose to love; that is an act of your will. Sexual attraction is another matter. A question I will ask God someday is why he made sexual drive so potent. Why did you do that, God?"

After lunch, I went home thinking to myself that God had put this man in my life to challenge me to use what I had learned and not to take my wife for granted. To value her and not underestimate her influence in my life. Falling in love is easy, but staying in love is hard. The fairy tale ends in marriage; no one wants to see what

2. Goodstein, "Marriage Gone Bad," paras. 2–3, 5.

3 Goodstein, "Marriage Gone Bad," para. 8.

happens next. Getting married does not mean you are ready. You can ruin your chance of being happy and fulfilled in life; passion seeps out when we lose our focus. It is not easy, but you must master the urge so as not to be distracted and lose your focus. We stay focused when we talk with, connect with, and respect each other.

A couple of days later, we were doing breakfast at Pancake House in Boca Raton one midweek morning. They made a cheese omelet that resembled a mushroom cloud. When served, it tasted awesome. When we were done, we walked down a couple of doors to a frozen-yogurt place. After we ordered, we sat outside at a small patio table, and we ate our frozen yogurt and talked some more. While we were sitting there, a young woman pulled up in a new BMW and parked near the curb in a no-parking zone. She ran into a woman's boutique store. The senior citizen who was parked legally started to back out of his parking space. The last time he had looked, there had been no car behind him. After he backed into this young woman's car, all hell broke loose. She heard the crash and came running out of the store screaming obscenities. Only a couple minutes had passed from when she left her car and entered the store to when the man backed into her car.

Dion, to his credit, jumped up and ran over and took total charge of the situation with compassion and authority. He walked her through every step of reporting an accident and prepared her to expect a summons for parking illegally. Watching this unfold, I was surprised, because I had not expected him to react in this manner. We have been taught for centuries to mind our own business. The Greek philosopher Epictetus is credited with saying, "Keep your attention focused entirely on what is truly your own concern, and be clear that what belongs to others is their business and none of yours."[4]

The young woman had no idea who it was that was helping her, nor was she in the right frame of mind to thank him afterwards. He got involved anonymously and left the same way. It was that event that sealed my commitment to becoming a licensed addiction counselor. Dion was not putting on a show for me or

4. Epictetus, "Keep your attention . . ."

anyone else. Getting involved in the lives of people around him is something he does automatically.

The following week, we met for Italian food at Nino's. After we ordered, I began our conversation by congratulating him on a newspaper article I had read that said they were making a movie about him. He did not say anything. I said, "Oh no, here is the article." He glanced at it, smiled at me, and said, "Eddy, your problem is that you believe everything you read." Our food was served: lasagna with side orders of meatballs and bread. The conversation continued with the question "Do I take what I read at face value and believe that the way things appear is the way they really are?" We covered everything from current events to the latest diet craze to theology. I thought by now that I was an authority on the subject until Dion started talking about the faith of the early fathers.

He would be the first to tell you he is not a scholar, he is not a theologian, and he is not an intellectual, just a student.

I know now that God put him in my life at the time to challenge me. I was going through a dry period then, hearing many voices saying "This is right" and "This is wrong." I was getting bored. I needed a fresh perspective of God's church—rather than focusing just on the four walls of my home—being mindful that error never enters the room by itself. It is always piggybacked on truth.

CHAPTER 14

Living Proof

A DVD OF DION live in concert was about to be released. He invited Wendi and I over to his home to see it. Wendi was going to meet Susan for the first time. They both welcomed her into their home with warmth and refreshments; you could feel the peacefulness in their home that immediately disarmed you. I was so concerned about them making a good impression on Wendi, because they were my friends and mature in their faith, and I liked them very much. Sometimes, we are just sleepwalking through life, completely unaware of the extraordinary people, moments, and possibilities that surround us. When that happens, life loses its flavor.

After having breakfast one morning, Dion and I were sitting in his Lexus listening to some songs I had recorded and some songs he had recorded but had not released yet. As we shared our music, I mentioned to him that I was looking for a recording studio that was local. He suggested I consider going to where he recorded. He said it was just down the street. It is funny, because he likes to say that a lot—he lives "just down the street," the recording studio is "just down the street," he goes to meetings "just down the street." Well, it was just down the street! I was serious about recording some new songs. Booking studio time and putting together musicians is not an easy task.

Besides working a management position, which required me to work a minimum of fifty hours a week, I also was going to school three nights a week, I facilitated a faith-based program and was a worship leader at my church, and I had a family. I had to find time for a recording project. But I knew that if I didn't do this, I would regret it years later.

Once you get past the initial excitement of being in a recording studio, you realize you have a project to do and a time frame to do it in. You should have every song mapped out—how you want it to go. If you do not, it is like trying to find the light switch in the dark, and that could become very costly. The first step is creating a guide for other instruments to follow along. Second step: record the rhythm section. As any musician knows, the rhythm section is the foundation of any song. When bands play together, everyone follows the drums and bass. The third thing is recording the harmonies and then recording the melodies and then background vocals, percussion, piano fills, and then sound effects.

I scheduled a time to record. Bob Guertin's Sounds Great Productions recording studio was the perfect place for me to record. Professionalism with creativity is how I describe my experience. I was very satisfied with the product. I had all the songs—complete except for my vocals—on a CD, which I gave Dion. I did that in case he heard a song he liked and wanted to experiment with it. A week later, we met, and afterward, Dion asked me to come over his house late in the week to put together an idea for a song he had in mind.

A few days later, I went over to his house with some lyrics I had written pertaining to his idea for a song. While I was sitting there looking around at all the gold records on the walls in his office, I began to feel intimidated. I stopped myself from looking through the prism of time and convinced myself that this was just two friends putting a song together, like I had done so many other times with other friends, and I stopped wondering if I was even good enough to be in the same room with him.

In your dreams as a young guy, you imagine your hero to be one thing and then you get a chance to spend time with them and find out that they are so much more. Deep down, I think that all rock and roll musicians/songwriters, at the end of their lives, would like to have written a song as good and true as one of Dion's lesser-known songs.

Afterward, Dion was thoughtful and kind enough to suggest I call Heart Beat Records to see if they might be able to help in getting some exposure for my album *Living Proof*.

Heart Beat Records was gracious in giving me half an hour on their Backstage series, which is broadcast on EWTN. I was picked up at Birmingham-Shuttlesworth International Airport and driven to the EWTN studios. That weekend, they were taping several different shows for the network. Over the next couple of days, all the guests involved met in the dining room for their meals. To sit with Marcus Grodi and Father Mitch Pacwa at one of the dining-room tables and hear them share personal stories of faith was an honor. I overheard one of the guests—I don't know his name—share the following story, which took place at a trunk-or-treat event in place of Halloween:

> "I was a Catholic once," said the lady a few yards from me in the parking lot. "Now I am a Christian, and you can be one as well!" She proceeded to hand the track to a gentleman standing next to the open trunk of his car.
>
> I could not help it. "Excuse me," I said to the lady, "but could I, too, have a track?"
>
> The lady's face beamed. She asked, "Are you saved?"
>
> "Of course I am. I am a believing Catholic," I said.
>
> She looked at me as if I had bad breath or something. She continued, "I was just telling this gentleman that I, too, was Catholic—a Catholic for thirty years, in fact. Now I have found Christ, and I am trying to tell everyone I know about salvation through Christ."
>
> "Wow, that is really something. May I ask why you left the church?" I could tell that my asking this question was making my new acquaintance excited. After all, she had probably been snubbed by dozens of people, and

now she had someone to whom she could witness about Christ. I did not care much, but I tried not to show it.

"You see," she said, "I was born a Catholic. I attended Mass every week, received the sacraments, and graduated from a Catholic school. Not once did I ever hear the gospel proclaimed. Not once! It was after the birth of my first child that a good friend of mine shared the gospel with me and I accepted Jesus as my personal Lord and Savior and became a Christian. Now I belong to a Bible-believing church, and I am sharing the gospel with whoever will listen."

This shocked me. "You mean you belonged to the Catholic Church for over forty years and you never heard the gospel?"

She was getting more excited. "Yes, I never once heard the gospel of salvation preached or taught or even mentioned in the church. If you do not preach the gospel—excuse my bluntness—you are simply not a Christian."

I scratched my head and said, "That is strange. I have been a Catholic all my life, and I bet I heard the gospel every week at church." My smile quickly changed into a look of curiosity. "Maybe I am missing something," I continued. "Tell me what you mean by the gospel."

The lady reached back into her purse to pull out a little track and said, "This track explains the simple gospel of salvation. It can be broken down into four easy steps.First, we acknowledge that we are all sinners in need of God's forgiveness. Secondly, we recognize that only God can save us. The third step is recognizing that Jesus Christ died on the cross for our sins to bring us to God. The fourth and final step is for each individual to accept Jesus Christ as their personal Lord and Savior, to be saved."

I thought for a couple of seconds and said, "If I could demonstrate to you that Catholics hear the gospel every Sunday, would you agree to take a closer look at the Catholic Church?"

Now she knew she had me over a barrel. "Prove it," she said.

I excused myself for a second and ran to my car to grab a Catholic missal. "Since you have attended Mass nearly all your life, you probably remember these prayers." I flipped open to the beginning prayers of the Mass and proceeded to show her how Catholics here pray and live the gospel message every Sunday.

The first step in my newfound friend's track stated that we all are sinners in need of God's forgiveness. After the greeting, the Mass continues to what is known as the "Penitential Act." I read aloud the text to her while she followed, reading silently: "I confess to almighty God and to you, my brothers and sisters, that I have greatly sinned, in my thoughts and in my words, in what I have done and in what I have failed to do."[1]

I mentioned that it is here in this section that each Catholic states publicly that he or she is individually a sinner, not merely in a general sense but specifically in thoughts, words, and deeds. You cannot get much more complete than that. I continued reading, and I asked the blessing: "I ask blessed Mary ever-Virgin, all the Angels and Saints, and you, my brothers and sisters, to pray for me to the Lord our God."[2] The priest reaffirms this confession of sin by praying, "May almighty God have mercy on us, forgive us our sins and bring us to everlasting life." And the whole congregation says, "Amen."[3]

I looked at her and said, "You see, we Catholics start every Mass with a public declaration of our own personal sinfulness and look to God for forgiveness."

She responded, "But Catholics do not believe that God alone can save them. They believe that Mary and the saints will save them."

I shook my head in disagreement. "No, we do not. Remember what we just read in the Mass. Catholics ask Mary, the angels, the saints, and the whole congregation to pray to God for mercy on their behalf. Just like I would ask you to pray for me to God—that does not mean that I look to you to save me. No, of course I do not believe

1. St. Norbert College, "Prayers for Mass," ll. 1–5.
2. St. Norbert College, "Prayers for Mass," ll. 8–11.
3. Thiron, "Penitential Act." paras. 11–12.

that. I am just asking for your help. Besides, the 'Gloria' of the Mass proves that Catholics look to God alone to save us. In the second century, Saint Justin Martyr wrote a letter to the Romans explaining how the early Christians worship. We use the same Mass today."

My experience at EWTN was wonderful. Everyone I met was open and friendly to me. What struck me was the genuineness of everyone.

The first Sunday back, I attended my evangelical church service. One of the congregants came up to me and said he had seen me while channel surfing. He had come across me on the program Backstage on EWTN Network and wanted to know why I was on a Catholic program. It was almost like it was sacrilegious to evangelicals. I had known this man for fifteen years. He was my brother in the Lord. He was part of my extended family—so was everyone else at that church. I suddenly began to remember what God had spoken to my heart on the plane back from Israel. "Stop alienating my church," he had said. For the next couple of years, I had considered myself a closet Catholic. Catholic means universal Christian church—the whole body of Christians collectively. My concern was about who has the authority to interpret Scripture and be able to see truth. I had in my home fifteen or more commentaries from many different pastors, some intellectuals, some scholars. They all agree on the basics, but on other matters they do not.

Chapter 15

Why Are We Prone to Get Addicted?

During this time, I was studying to prepare to take the exam to be able to work in the mental health field. The day of the test, I was upstairs in my bathroom combing my hair, and I whispered to God, "Could you be with me today?" I was not anxious or stressed, I just did not want to do it alone. In a very general way, God reminded me in a flash of all the times he had been with me and had never left me. I had just forgotten the journey.

It was a fifty-mile trip down to Miami to take the three-hour exam. I wept all the way there and all the way back. I have learned that you cannot be in the presence of God and not shed a tear.

After I got home, Wendi asked me how I did on the exam. I had no idea. I had never taken an exam like that. Even all the pretests had not prepared me for this. I would get my license in the mail if I passed.

One week later, my license was in the mailbox. I was joyful, and everyone else who supported me was also joyful.

A short time later, I began working at a mental health facility. The patients were homeless and addicted to opiates but were now being given therapy and housing. I was hired as a group therapist with thirty patients who were suffering from a dual diagnosis of schizophrenia and drug addiction. In a lot of cases, the family severs ties with the patients. Individuals with schizophrenia usually have difficulty keeping a job and caring for themselves. They must rely on family and friends for help. The disease is often misunderstood, but it is treatable, and in many cases, the individual can go on to lead a productive and normal life, providing they stay on their medication. According to an article published in *BMC Med*, "Early treatment discontinuation on the part of patients with schizophrenia or schizophrenia-like disorders is strikingly common, with estimates of its prevalence in antipsychotic drug trials ranging from 25%–75%."[1] There are many variables, but the most common drug addiction is that the patient feels that illegal drugs normalize them. Because of the chemical imbalance that happens when they stop taking the prescribed medication, they enter a danger zone. According to Medical News Today, "A chemical imbalance in the brain occurs when a person has either too little or too much of certain neurotransmitters. Neurotransmitters are the chemical messengers that pass information between nerve cells. Examples of neurotransmitters include serotonin, dopamine, and norepinephrine."[2]

According to Medical News Today, "People sometimes refer to dopamine and serotonin as the 'happy hormones' due to the roles they play in regulating mood and emotion."[3] A popular hypothesis is that mental health disorders such as depression and anxiety develop as a result of chemical imbalances in the brain. Other factors that contribute to mental health conditions include genetics; family history; life experiences such as a history of physical, psychological, or emotional abuse; and having a history of alcohol or illicit drugs.[4]

In the very first book of the Old Testament, God blesses Adam and Eve and says to them, "Be fruitful and increase in number; fill the earth and subdue it" (Gen 1:28). This is a divine order to our physical bodies. Any disruption to how that order flows

---

1. Liu-Seifert et al., "Treatment of Schizophrenic Patients," para. 5.

2. Eske, "Chemical Imbalances," paras. 1–2.

3. Eske, "Dopamine and Serotonin," 1–2.

4. See Eske, "Dopamine and Serotonin."

could eventually be harmful or disastrous. God created us with neurotransmitters and endorphins so that when we accomplish a goal and get a desired result, endorphins are released. Since endorphins act on the opioid receptors in our brains, they reduce pain and boost pleasure. It is when we corrupt the natural order of how our bodies function that we get into serious problems. With drug and alcohol addiction, we try to get that feeling of euphoria without earning it. Our bodies are designed to follow a pattern, a very balanced state of mental steadiness. Drug addiction counteracts that balance of mental steadiness, resulting in cravings for the drug of your choice. Everyone who engages in addictive behavior will experience uncomfortable cravings and urges at the outset of recovery that can be very intense. But they will subside if you can wait it out until the chemicals in your body begin to balance out and the body begins to be normalized.

We were created by God to work well only when we are in union with him. As Dion says, "To know God is to be fully alive as a human being. A broken mind cannot fix itself." I was a drug addict from ages fourteen to thirty. By age twenty-three, I had been in the two worst state prisons in New York, Sing Sing and Dannemora, with a life sentence hanging over my head. I reached out to God and said, "If you're real, come into my life. I need you." Now, forty years later, I have not had a drink or a drug since. The most courageous thing we can do is open our hearts to our Creator. God is not a concept to be understood but a person to be encountered in the depth of one's being.

Chapter 16

An Encounter with Beauty

IN MARCH OF 2003, the United States was fighting in Iraq, our son Phillip was deployed, and as a result, our daughter-in-law moved with our grandchildren to East Tennessee to be closer to her mom and dad. She needed their support and the environment of country living for her children and peace of mind. The United States Army was preparing her husband to fight in a war, and she was a wreck.

We made many trips to East Tennessee during this time. The town was exceedingly small—less than fifteen hundred people—with mountains all around. The country courthouse sat in the middle of town on Main Street. It was a very picturesque setting as you drove into town, and it appeared to be a very charming place to live. The country was very rural, with farmland stretched out for hundreds of acres. Much of the landscape was peppered more with homesteads with farm buildings than communities filled with families.

Many times when leaving the small town, we would pass Veterans Overlook on Clinch Mountain. You were so high up that the panoramic view of Cherokee Lake and the surrounding hills was spectacular. It made you cry out that God was responsible for so much beauty. Eventually, we grew very fond of East Tennessee, so much that we even purchased some land. I entertained the thought of being a home builder and thought about building plans and cost factors. It was extremely easy for me to fantasize and indulge myself in imagining what it would be like to create our own homestead on Yellow Branch Rd. But we decided that the timing was not right yet to take on such a big undertaking. We had learned that when you move to another state, like we did when we moved from Brooklyn to Florida, there are a lot of things that must line up economically, medically, and—most importantly—spiritually. In Isa 60:22, God says, "I am the Lord; in its time I will do this swiftly." Sometimes, the way God builds my faith is to disappoint my expectations.

During the waiting period, I investigated financial aspects of moving to Tennessee. Homeowners insurance, car insurance, city and state taxes. I had heard reassuring things over the years, but I wanted to make doubly sure so that when we got older, we would not have to work unless we wanted to. There is an old person down inside of all of us that is dependent on us to be wise and prepare for the future. Do not disappoint that person by being foolish through the strongest, most productive years of your life.

Several months had passed when the company I worked for announced they were opening a new district in Knoxville, Tennessee. It was wonderful to hear that they were going to relocate to Knoxville. Now we had to put our house on the market to sell. Our faith is what got us through the ups and downs of selling our home and relocating to another state. In a little over a year after renting in Tennessee, we were in our new home. Wendi and I both agreed that when you do everything solely for your benefit in life, it dies with you, but everything you do selflessly will continue to positively influence others for a long time to come.

"Let us not become weary in doing good, for at the proper time we will reap a harvest if we do not give up" (Gal 6:9). "As long as the earth endures, seedtime and harvest, cold and heat, summer and winter, day and night will never cease" (Gen 8:22). These are truths that are written in the Bible. "Do not be deceived: God cannot be mocked. A man reaps what he sows" (Gal 6:7). If a farmer plants seeds of lettuce, he does not get carrots. So it is with everything we sow. If we sow hatred, we will not reap love. If anything, it would be resentment, hostility, or retribution.

You cannot eliminate habits that no longer serve you. You can only replace them with new habits that support your goals. Moment by moment, you need to live with awareness and create positive habits. Behavior modification programs do not work. We need grace as an operational system to sustain long-time change in our lives. One of the big takeaways from the story of the prodigal son (Luke 15:11–32) is that after the son came to his senses, he had something to come home to.

A lot of times, there is nothing to come home to. Family members are emotionally, financially, and spiritually drained. Family members are not equipped for the crisis of a loved one being addicted to alcohol and drugs. They cannot handle this by themselves. A support group like Al-Anon or a local church that will support them without condemnation is an avenue that will prove to be extremely helpful.

CHAPTER 17

Michael's Story[1]

GOD DOES NOT SEE your life as you see it; he sees it in reverse, and he already sees you free. So he says that you are free, because he sees that you are free even when you do not feel free!

As I look back over my forty-year journey through life thus far, there have been countless times when God's hand over my life has been quite evident. The first five years or so were spent in hospital rooms sick from an illness for which doctors had no answers. Desperation was all my mom and dad knew at that time. By my parents asking for God's healing hand in my life, I was miraculously touched; that night, it was made known that there must be a greater purpose in store for me. Throughout the next eighteen years, I somehow forgot the work that had been started in me.

Like every other teenager, with a chip on my shoulder, I became rebellious. I started running around with a local street gang and experimenting with alcohol and drugs, mainly cocaine and heroin. I felt tough and untouchable. It is crazy to think about what we tell ourselves when we step out from under the umbrella of God's protection. Well, the lifestyle I was leading placed me in the Broward County Detention Center for the first time at nineteen.

1. This chapter was written by my son Michael.

I will be honest—when that cell door slammed behind me, it was as if every ounce of toughness was drained from my body. I was frightened at what the outcome would be. Somehow, I made it out of that with no consequences. Little did I know that this would not be the last time I would experience the inside of a jail cell. From then on, I had people hanging over my shoulder telling me things like "You have a problem" and "You need to get straight." I just wanted to be left alone. I did not think I had a problem. I thought I could quit anytime. It was everyone else who had the problem, not me, I thought. Six months later, I did the only thing I could think of to get my parents, family members, and some friends off my back. I checked myself into an inpatient rehabilitation center in Fort Lauderdale, Florida. I went in thinking I would get this over with in nine months, no problem, and then I would finally be left alone. God had another idea in mind, and it was not the plan I chose.

I had only been a resident of the facility for a short time when God's presence just broke me one evening. I tried fighting it, but I had no other choice except to give in. I started to give this a second thought. Maybe living for him was the better route and a much better idea. Praying and reading the Bible became a daily routine for me for the remainder of my time there. But it was not a heartfelt decision I wanted to keep. I still had other ideas in mind when I walked out of there six months later.

In February of 2001, I left and remained sober for the next four months, making it to an entire year of staying clean. Unfortunately, the damage had already been done. The cycle had started with that first drink, that first pill, that first experience. I had always been told while growing up in the church that the enemy would not tie you up if he were not afraid of what would happen if you got loose. I agree with that and have seen that to be so true in my life. I went right back to living for that high. It had become too difficult for me to be honest and live for Christ and give him my failures and struggles. For fourteen years—despite several doctors, a therapist, medications, and numerous people trying to help me live in a better way—I was on a downward spiral.

By the time I reached thirty years old, my hard work with the company I had been with for some time had paid off. I was promised a position of authority that would enable me to be at the top of my profession. The enticements that come with having more money in your pocket quickly overtook me. In just a short time, I had moved into a luxury apartment just a short distance from the beach and bought myself a new car and all the things money could buy. Oddly enough, nothing satisfied me, gave me contentment, or made me feel complete. Was God still trying to gain my attention? I felt that all the areas of my life were filled. I had the position, I had the stuff, I had the girl, and I was involved with a successful rock band. The more I had, the emptier I felt. How could that be? An old friend puts it this way: it is as if you are trying to fill a God-sized hole in your heart with things that were never meant to take the place of your Savior. But the bottle was still the most important thing in my life, or—what I used to refer to it as—my best friend.

My drinking and use of drugs very quickly escalated from that point on, and I did not have a sober breath for another five years. In just a short time, the well had dried up. The position was gone, the home was gone, the car was gone. Rather than end up homeless and jobless, I took the hit to my pride and ask Mom and Dad for help. The plan was to move to East Tennessee and get sober and start a new life. Who did I think I was fooling? I was an alcoholic, and there was no way I was giving up the bottle or the girl. I was looking for a bailout with no accountability.

I learned exceedingly early on that you can change locations, but if you do not change behavior, things will not change in your life. Deep down in the pit of my spirit, I wanted the change; I wanted the fresh start; I wanted a relationship with my Creator—but physically, I could not stop. After just under two years of being a Tennessee resident, everything came crashing down on top of me. The inside of a jail cell became a revolving door, several jobs were lost due to my alcoholism and drug addiction, the girl was gone for good, and tears filled the sleepless nights. After two more apartment evictions, I finally left to move back in with Mom and Dad. My time had run out, and I was done. Late one evening as I stood there outside of my parents' home in tears while trying to drink myself to the point of suicide, a peaceful, still voice came up within me out of nowhere. Even now, how could God still want to reach me? I will never forget those peaceful words of encouragement he said to me in that moment: "Michael, I love you. I have always been here. Give me your heart, failure, and pain, and I will give you rest and a life beyond your understanding."

I said, "If you love me that much, God, then prove yourself, and maybe I'll consider what you are asking!" Not only did he prove himself, but he went above and beyond what I had asked. Seek, knock, believe, and have faith. The simple words of a prayer, but my deliverance would not take place for another two weeks.

November 16, 2015, was just like any other night, except this one would be different from the rest. In a drunken haze, I completely gave up and stopped fighting once and for all. I dropped to my knees and said a simple prayer: "I cannot do this on my own anymore. Please help me." In that moment, he did for me what I could not do for myself. My life has never been the same since, and I have not had a drug or a drink since that night, by his grace. This time was genuine. This time was heartfelt.

I found myself one week later in a room filled with people who were just like me, who thought just like me and behaved like me, but who had made their way out of a destructive lifestyle through a spiritually based twelve-step program. I regularly started meetings with these people, who talked about how to become better fathers, better husbands, better sons, better members of society. I was living in a way I had never known before. Looking back on those first few months or even that first year, I am now able to see that God really had been in my life the whole time—through every struggle, through good and bad, through every victory, in every area of my life.

Today, I live a life of gratitude by giving back to others what has been freely given to me. Sharing the good word of hope, love, forgiveness, and recovery is what brings joy in my life. I am a firm believer in sharing God's goodness and grace, in saying that what he has done for me, he can and will do for you.

God does not see your life as you see it. He sees it in reverse, and he already sees you free. So he says that you are free, because he sees that you are free, even when you do not feel free!

CHAPTER 18

Naaman

SOMETIMES THE HEALING YOU receive is not necessarily in the way you planned it would happen. Naaman was truly a great man, but he was afflicted with a grievous skin disease. As this story unfolds in the Old Testament, Elisha, the man of God, heard about Naaman and what had happened when Naaman was sent to the king of Israel to get healed. The king of Israel had gotten incredibly angry that he was expected to heal Naaman. Elisha heard what had happened and sent word to the king. He said, "Have the man come to me and he will know that there is a prophet in Israel" (2 Kgs 5:8).

So Naaman stopped at Elisha's door. Elisha sent out a servant to meet him with this message: "Go, wash yourself seven times in the Jordan, and your flesh will be restored and you will be cleansed" (2 Kgs 5:9).

Naaman lost his temper. He turned on his heels, saying, "I thought that he would surely come out to me and stand and call on the name of the Lord his God, wave his hand over the spot and cure me of my leprosy. Are not Abana and Pharpar, the rivers of Damascus, better than all the waters of Israel? Couldn't I wash in them and be cleansed?" (2 Kgs 5:11–12). He stomped off mad as a hornet.

But his servants caught up with him and said, "My father, if the prophet had told you to do some great thing, would you not have done it? How much more, then, when he tells you, 'Wash and be cleansed'!" (2 Kgs 5:13).

So he did it. He went down and immersed himself in the Jordan River seven times, following the orders of the holy man.

Naaman's skin was healed. His skin was now like the skin of a little baby. He was as good as new. He then went back to the holy man with his entourage and, standing before Elisha, said, "Now I know that there is no God in all the world except in Israel" (2 Kgs 5:15).

I have learned that you limit God by putting him in a box or by thinking you have a formula to get God to answer your wish list. When I have humbled myself and had a sense of humility about how little I can do and how great God is, things have started to change for the better. If doctors find a cure that heals you, it does not negate the fact that God healed you of your disease. This does not cause God's healing to lose its value.

Make sure your worst enemy is not living between your own two ears. As the title of Ronnie D. Henderson's book puts it, "The me I see is the me I will be."[1] You have a brain in your head and feet in your shoes. Get moving—God will lead you. Listen to his voice. We all walk on different paths, which means it is useless to compare our own road to someone else's.

---

1. Henderson, *Me I See*.

Chapter 19

In the Arms of the Angels

"Would you tell me, please, which way I ought to go from here?" was the question Alice asked the Cheshire Cat.

He answered, "That depends a good deal on where you want to get to."

Alice replied that it did not matter much. The Cheshire Cat responded, "Then it doesn't matter which way you go."[1]

In other words, if you do not know where you are going, any road will get you there.

That is exactly what I was facing forty-five years ago standing on a Route 86 sidewalk near Dannemora. And then, many years later, in 2019, I was back for our forty-year anniversary—standing in the same place, reflecting on the journey, considering what mattered and what did not, and eventually, shining a light on the person I had become and the person I was yet to be.

Wendi and I decided that for our fortieth anniversary we would rent a huge log cabin near Lake Placid, New York. We would invite our sons and their families to reminisce about the many camping trips we had experienced up there in the Adirondack Mountains. To help us with that, we invited Diana and Keith, who

1. Carroll, *Alice's Adventures in Wonderland*, 71–72.

were much more than dear friends—they were family. The friends we choose are a clear reflection of us as individuals. They are the people that can inspire us to accomplish much. My mother used to say, "Show me your friends, and I will tell you who you are."

I spent most of my life having intense trust issues. Quite a lot of times, I have been disappointed by friends and loved ones. In fact, I have let myself down from time to time. Christianity is not a kind of cosmetic surgery so we can hide imperfections. You cannot hide what you have been through. Forgiveness does not mean the thing never happened. Jesus forgave those who crucified him on the cross. But when doubting Thomas wanted proof, Jesus stood before him, still with scars. The nails were gone, but the scars were still there; they had not faded away. Jesus says to forgive every time we remember the hurt that people have caused. Please do not buy into the claim that if you truly have forgiven, you will not remember. In my life, I refuse to blame someone forever for any negative advantage they took over me.

There is a Buddhist parable that goes as follows:

> The story goes that two monks were traveling together, a senior and a junior. They came to a river with a strong current where a young woman was waiting, unable to cross alone. She asks the monks if they would help her across the river. Without a word and in spite of the sacred vow he'd taken not to touch women, the older monk picks her up, crosses, and sets her down on the other side.
>
> The younger monk joins them across the river and is aghast that the older monk has broken his vow but doesn't say anything. An hour passes as they travel on. Then two hours. Then three. Finally, the now quite agitated younger monk can stand it no longer: "Why did you carry that women [sic] when we took a vow as monks not to touch women?"
>
> The older monk replies, "I set her down hours ago by the side of the river. Why are you still carrying her?"
>
> The story is a reminder to not dwell on the past in a way that interferes with living in the present moment.[2]

---

2. Kottke, "Story of Two Monks," paras. 2–5.

Redemption in Brooklyn

I am sure I am not alone as a musician in that when it comes to playing piano or guitar, I must play every day. It moves me into a peaceful zone out of the craziness of this world in which we live. I do this totally for enjoyment. Recently, I was sitting down at the piano playing the song "Angel" by Sarah McLachlan. It is such a moving melody that I began to wonder what motivated her to write this beautiful song that so touches the soul.

I found out that Sarah was reading a story about a keyboard player for the group Smashing Pumpkins who died from a drug overdose. The person who was with him in the Regency Hotel in New York had brought a very potent form of heroin from the Lower East Side of Manhattan. After intravenously injecting themselves with the heroin, the keyboard player was not responsive to his bandmate's nudging. The bandmate tried to revive him by dragging him into a cold shower fully clothed, but to no avail.[3] He died, leaving behind a wife and four-month-old son. He was thirty-four years old.[4] A very tragic story that continues to repeat itself; the parade of names is endless.

In 1978, shortly before I met Wendi, this same thing happened to me in an apartment on Avenue H and Cortelyou Road in Brooklyn. I had totally forgotten—this had taken place some forty-two years earlier. I was so humbled and grateful to still be alive. All that happened after I met Wendi would not have taken place had I become just another statistic of drug overdose.

The movie *It's a Wonderful Life* comes to mind. George Bailey has so many problems, he is thinking about ending it all, and it is Christmas. As George is about to jump from a bridge, he ends up rescuing his guardian angel, Clarence Odbody, who then shows George what his town would look like if it had not been for all his good deeds over the years.[5]

Hindsight, it has been said, is twenty-twenty. In hindsight, we all would have done things differently, but in the moment, we do not have the clarity to understand what is happening. My dad

3. Strauss, "Musician for Smashing Pumpkins."
4. "Pumpkins Pay Widow," para. 3.
5. Capra, *It's a Wonderful Life*.

used to say to me all the time, "Eddy, do not take chances." I did not understand that concept until much later in life. My guardian angel must have worked a lot of overtime with me.

At times, I felt unimportant and ineffective, like I had no value, was good for nothing, and no one would miss me if I were gone. I felt invisible. But when I found out there is a God in heaven who wants to be involved in my daily life to the point of finding me irresistible, things changed. I was no longer alone. Suddenly, I realized I was valued, that I had a purpose for being on this earth, at this time, and this place.

Bibliography

Barron, Robert. "Tuesday, March 22, 2022." https://www.wordonfire.org/reflections/lent/c-lent-wk3-tuesday/.

"Best Kibbutz Hotels." https://www.touristisrael.com/best-kibbutz-hotels/3825/.

"Brown v. Board and 'The Doll Test'." https://www.naacpldf.org/brown-vs-board/significance-doll-test/.

"Caesarea Philippi." https://www.bibleplaces.com/caesarea-philippi-banias/.

Capra, Frank, dir. *It's a Wonderful Life*. 131 min. RKO Radio Pictures, 1946.

Carroll, Lewis. *Alice's Adventures in Wonderland*. New York: Random House, 1946.

Carroll, Melissa. "Then and Now: The Evolution of Treatments for Hepatitis C." April 15, 2019. https://www.healthline.com/health/hepatitis-c/evolution-of-treatments.

Centers for Disease Control and Prevention. "Viral Hepatitis." https://www.cdc.gov/hepatitis/hcv/cfaq.htm.

Einstein, Albert. "Coincidence is God's . . ." brainyquote.com/quotes/albert_einstein_574924.

Epictetus. "Keep your attention . . ." https://libquotes.com/epictetus/quote/lbfog8i.

Eske, Jamie. "Dopamine and Serotonin: Brain Chemicals Explained." August 19, 2019. https://www.medicalnewstoday.com/articles/326090.

———. "Everything You Need to Know about Chemical Imbalances in the Brain." September 26, 2019. https://www.medicalnewstoday.com/articles/326475.

Gilbert, Derek P. "Mount Hermon and the Mesopotamian Origin of the Watchers." April 21, 2017. Video, 7:17. https://www.derekpgilbert.com/2017/04/21/mount-hermon-and-the-mesopotamian-origin-of-the-watchers/.

Bibliography

Goodstein, Laurie. "A Marriage Gone Bad Struggles for Redemption." *New York Times*, October 29, 1997. https://www.nytimes.com/1997/10/29/us/a-marriage-gone-bad-struggles-for-redemption.html.

Henderson, Ronnie D. *The Me I See Is the Me I'll Be: Understanding Our Identity.* Bloomington, IN: WestBow, 2018.

Kottke, Jason. "The Story of Two Monks and a Woman." January 26, 2020. https://kottke.org/20/01/the-story-of-two-monks-and-a-woman.

Liu-Seifert, Hong, et al. "Discontinuation of Treatment of Schizophrenic Patients Is Driven by Poor Symptom Response: A Pooled Post-hoc Analysis of Four Atypical Antipsychotic Drugs." *BMC Med* 3 (2005). https://doi.org/10.1186/1741-7015-3-21.

Nee, Watchman. *Spiritual Authority.* New York: Christian Fellowship, 1972.

"Pumpkins Pay Widow of Overdosed Musician." *Chicago Tribune*, October 22, 1997. https://www.chicagotribune.com/news/ct-xpm-1997-10-22-9710220072-story.html.

"RKO Madison Theatre." http://cinematreasures.org/theaters/4621.

"Sacco & Vanzetti: Who Were Sacco & Vanzetti?" https://www.mass.gov/info-details/sacco-vanzetti-who-were-sacco-vanzetti.

St. Norbert College. "Prayers for Mass." https://www.snc.edu/parish/prayers-for-mass-1.pdf.

Strauss, Neil. "Musician for Smashing Pumpkins Dies of Apparent Drug Overdose." *New York Times*, July 13, 1996. https://www.nytimes.com/1996/07/13/nyregion/musician-for-smashing-pumpkins-dies-of-apparent-drug-overdose.html.

Thiron, Rita. "The Roman Missal: The Penitential Act." *Faith*, April 2011. https://faithmag.com/roman-missal-penitential-act.

"Types of Mental Health Problems." https://www.mind.org.uk/information-support/types-of-mental-health-problems/.

Twain, Mark. "I am an old . . ." https://www.brainyquote.com/quotes/mark_twain_108600.

Wilson, Aaron D. "Rockefeller Drug Laws Information Sheet." https://www.prdi.org/rocklawfact.html.